CHRISTMAS BAKING

Christian Teubner

Christmas Baking

Traditional Recipes Made Easy

BARRON'S

First English-language edition published 1985 by Barron's
Educational Series, Inc.

© 1983 by Gräfe und Unzer GmbH, Munich, West Germany

The title of the German edition is *Weihnachtsbäckerei*.

All inquiries should be addressed to:
Barron's Educational Series, Inc.
250 Wireless Boulevard
Hauppauge, New York 11788

Library of Congress Catalog Card No. 85-13552

Cloth Edition
International Standard Book No. 0-8120-5617-5

Paper Edition
International Standard Book No. 0-8120-1372-7

Library of Congress Cataloging-in-Publication Data
Teubner, Christian.
        Christmas baking.

        Translation of Weihnachtsbäckerei.
        Includes index.
        1. Christmas cookery.   I. Title.
TX739.T4713   1985   641.8'65   85-13552
ISBN 0-8120-1372-7 (pbk)
ISBN 0-8120-5617-5

Color photographs by Christian Teubner

Translation and Americanization by Anne Mendelson

PRINTED IN HONG KONG
5   490   9876543

CONTENTS

BASIC BAKING TECHNIQUES

There are many reasons for doing your own baking at Christmas-time, but the most important is quality. This is a special time of the year and you want everything to be just right. Certainly the recipes in this book are not particularly difficult, but for successful results you should measure ingredients precisely and follow the instructions given. You'll have fun making these Christmas treats—and also experience the satisfaction of making top-quality goods.

No recipe can be written so precisely as to prevent occasional minor problems, however. One need only think of different baking temperatures and times. These can vary depending on your own oven; even with modern, up-to-date ovens there are often differences of 35° F. (20°C) or more between individual models, to say nothing of the differences presented with the newer convection ovens. For this reason, have an accurate oven thermometer handy, and refer to it frequently.

You should be especially careful handling doughs that have to be rolled out very thin—for example, most butter cookies and some Lebkuchen or honey cookies. Use the temperatures and baking times given in the recipes only as a general guide, and for complete certainty, test for doneness by baking two or three cookies first, before you do the whole batch.

Follow instructions closely for preparing these doughs and bat-ters, since these recipes have been thoroughly tested with these quantities. Cutting back even on such apparently minor points as resting intervals or chilling or drying periods often can make the difference between success and failure. Save yourself time and worry, and follow the instructions. There are times, however, when a little individual adjustment needs to be made. Flour, for example, varies greatly in its ability to absorb moisture. For example, a dough or batter that is too runny can be made firmer with a little more flour. A too-soft macaroon mixture can be worked better if more ground almonds are added to the dough. The same holds true for handling any cookie or cake dough, as well as for icing or coating with chocolate. First follow the suggested routine with a few cookies and wait to see the results; then take corrective action if, for example, an icing mixture is too stiff or the chocolate is too warm.

Ingredients: Use only the best, freshest, natural products. This applies particularly to butter, cream, and eggs, but one should also be careful with almonds and other nuts or candied lemon and orange peel; don't buy last year's goods. Freshness is especially hard to check with almonds, pistachios, and other nuts. They are often offered for sale already chopped, slivered, or sliced. Though prepared forms certainly are quite practical, stored nuts suf-fer somewhat as a result. Cooks who take the trouble to shell and chop their almonds or pistachios have a head start on quality. The same is true for candied lemon or orange peel sold pre-diced.

Almond Paste: Almond paste is used for many Christmas cookies and breads. You can make it yourself, but not with the quality of the modern commercial product. For this reason, the recipe directions refer to commercial almond paste.

Spices and Seasonings: Be choosy in buying spices, since they lose their aroma quickly. For grated orange or lemon rind, make it a point to use only unsprayed or untreated fruit (available in health food stores).

Chocolate: Chocolate can often become a source of vexation in Christmas baking when it is used to coat or decorate. If real chocolate is used—a semisweet cooking variety for melting—it usually becomes gray and unattractive-looking. If a chocolate-flavored coating is used instead, the result is more attractive but it doesn't compare with real chocolate in terms of flavor. A photo sequence on page 43 shows just how to handle chocolate correctly in order to preserve both its flavor and its glistening finish.

Timetable: Anyone who bakes for the holidays will certainly not be content with just one kind of cookie. For this reason, make yourself a little schedule of when to make one type or another. There are many types of cookies and cakes, from various honey cakes and cookies, to dried fruit breads; from dense-textured stollen to various macaroon recipes, marzipan potatoes, and lebkuchen. Many can be prepared several weeks before the holiday. In fact, baked specialties like Pfeffernüsse and Fruit Wedges demand a fairly long storage period to soften and mellow them. Many of the butter cookies can also stand up to a period of storage (or even be frozen, with some limitations). Others taste best fresh—and even better when you break the rules by eating them during Advent.

How to Make Sugar Syrups: Sugar is used in these recipes, not only in its regular granulated and superfine or powdered form, but also often in liquid form. For example, there are sugar glazes used in some Christmas baking. To make sugar liquid, the dry sugar must first be mixed with water; consistency will vary according to how much the water content of the mixture is reduced through boiling. The basic formula is to combine 2½ cups (500 g) superfine sugar with 1 quart (1 L) water. Boil this mixture until the sugar "clears"—that is, until it is completely dissolved in the water. After about 2-3 minutes, a light syrup will be produced, suitable for manifold uses in baking. If this solution is boiled another 5 min-

utes, you'll have a somewhat thicker sugar syrup, which will keep notably longer.

The next stage is extremely important for glazes: the "thread." For this the sugar syrup is further boiled to 220°F. (104°C) over low heat. For greatest accuracy, use a candy thermometer. Otherwise, wet your thumb and index finger with cold water, then very quickly dip out a bit of the sugar solution with your index finger. First touch together, then separate thumb and index finger. If a thin thread is formed, the right temperature has been reached.

Sugar in solution becomes even thicker when it is cooked to the "soft ball" stage. For this, the sugar is allowed to go on cooking over low heat to about 249°F. (116°C). This could also be measured without a thermometer. Dip out a little syrup with a cooking spoon, moisten thumb and index finger in ice water, take a little of the syrup between them, and dip again into ice water. If the solution can easily be rolled into a sphere or ball, the right temperature has been reached.

Glazing with Apricot Preserves and Fondant: Glazes make it possible to keep cakes and other baked goods moist and fresh for a longer period. To prepare a glaze, boil ¼ cup (50 g) of sugar with 2 jiggers (4 cL) water and 1 teaspoon lemon juice until the solution is clear. Then add ⅓ cup (100 g) apricot preserves and

cook down for about 4-5 minutes, stirring constantly. Brush the cookies or pastries with this apricot glaze, then allow to dry 10-15 minutes. To use fondant (plain sugar glaze), melt the sugar syrup in a bain-marie or double boiler and thin as necessary with a little egg white or lemon juice; apply in a thin coating over the cake.

Storing Christmas Cookies and Cakes: Remember that each variety of cookie should be packed in tins or boxes by itself; don't mix them together. Only in this way can each keep its individual flavor and crispness.

HONEY AND MOLASSES COOKIES

Brown Cookies

For about 60 cookies
⅔ cup (150 mL) molasses
2½ tablespoons honey
½ cup (100 g) lard
¾ cup (180 g) sugar
4 cups (500 g) all-purpose flour
2 teaspoons cinnamon
¼ teaspoon salt
1 teaspoon baking powder
½ teaspoon baking soda
2 eggs, lightly beaten
1⅓ cups (200 g) whole blanched almonds
1 cup (200 g) diced candied lemon peel
1 egg yolk

Combine molasses, honey, lard, and sugar in heavy saucepan. Place over medium-high heat and cook, while stirring occasionally, until mixture begins to foam and bubble. Remove from heat and let cool 15 minutes.

In a large bowl combine flour, cinnamon, salt, baking powder, and baking soda. Add whole eggs to molasses mixture; pour at once into flour mixture. Stir until a soft dough forms. Divide dough in half. Wrap each half separately in plastic wrap. Refrigerate at least 2 hours, or overnight.

Preheat the oven to 400°F. (200°C).

Roll out half piece of dough at a time on a heavily floured board to thickness of ⅛ inch (½ cm). Cut into rectangles about 2 × 3 inches (5 × 8 cm) in size. Place on greased baking sheet. Beat egg yolk with 2 teaspoons water. Brush cookies with egg mixture. Decorate tops of each cookie with an almond and a piece of candied lemon peel. Bake for 6 to 8 minutes, watching closely because cookies bake very quickly and may burn easily.

Variation: Brown Cookies with Chocolate Glaze

These are made by the same recipe as Brown Cookies, but not brushed with egg yolk or garnished with almonds. The cookies are cooled after baking and coated with tempered bittersweet cooking chocolate (see page 43). An especially thin coating can be achieved by applying the chocolate with a pastry brush. If you dip the whole cookie into the melted chocolate, you should tap off as much of the excess chocolate as possible and wipe the underside on the rim of the bowl. Place on parchment paper to let the coating harden, and garnish with almond halves and candied lemon peel before the chocolate is set.

Variation: Brown Cookies with Lemon Glaze

This sweet-tart glaze is outstandingly well suited to honey cookies. To make it, mix 2 tablespoons lemon juice and 1 jigger (2 cL) rum with 1 cup (100 g) confectioners sugar, sifted after measuring. The glaze should be very thin; add more lemon juice if necessary. The cookies are topped with almonds and baked as in the first recipe; they are coated with the glaze while still warm and allowed to dry completely on a wooden board or (preferably) a cake rack.

Chocolate Pfeffernüsse

Pfeffernüsse, or pepper-nuts, are among the oldest of Christmas baked specialties. They originated at a time when sugar was prohibitively expensive, consequently the sweetening was done predominately with honey.

For about 80 cookies
1 cup (250 g) honey
1/3 cup (100 g) molasses
1 cup (150 g) light brown sugar, measured without packing
1/2 cup (150 g) butter
4 cups (500 g) all-purpose flour
1/2 cup (50 g) sifted cocoa
1 teaspoon baking powder
1/4 teaspoon baking soda
1/4 teaspoon salt
1 teaspoon each cinnamon and white pepper
1/4 teaspoon mace
2 eggs
1/4 cup (50 g) diced candied lemon peel
3/4 cup (100 g) finely chopped blanched almonds
Grated rind of 1 lemon
1 1/2 pounds (700 g) semisweet chocolate

Combine honey, molasses, brown sugar, and butter in heavy saucepan. Place over medium-high heat and cook, stirring occasionally, until butter melts and mixture begins to bubble gently. Remove from heat and let cool 15 minutes. In large bowl combine flour, cocoa, baking powder, baking soda, salt, cinnamon, white pepper and mace. Add eggs to honey mixture, pour at once into flour mixture. Stir to form a dough. Add candied lemon peel, chopped almonds, and lemon rind; mix well. Divide dough in half. Wrap each half separately in plastic wrap. Refrigerate 1 1/2 hours, or overnight. Pinch off small pieces of dough (about heaping teaspoon size) and roll into balls. Place on greased baking sheets about 2 1/2 inches (5 cm) apart. Bake at 350°F. (180°C) for 12 to 15 minutes, or until done. Remove to racks to cool completely. Temper the chocolate as described on page 43. Dip cookies in melted chocolate and tap off excess on the rim of the bowl. Place on parchment paper or wax paper to dry.

Note: Pfeffernüse are traditionally made with potassium carbonate as the leavening. If you wish to make the cookies with this leavening, substitute 1 tablespoon potassium carbonate or 4 teaspoons single-acting baking powder for the baking powder and baking soda. Dissolve the potassium carbonate in 4 tablespoons cream or milk and add along with eggs.

Note: Potassium carbonate is a traditional leavening agent in German baking. It is available by mail order from the sources listed on page 94. Single-acting baking powder is available from some mail order sources, or you can make your own by combining baking soda with a pinch of cream of tartar.

Whole-Wheat Pfeffernüsse

For about 80 cookies
1 cup (250 g) honey
1 cup (150 g) light brown sugar, measured without packing
1/2 cup (200 g) butter
3 cups (400 g) whole-wheat flour
1 cup (150 g) all-purpose flour
1 teaspoon baking powder
1/4 teaspoon baking soda
1/4 teaspoon salt
2 teaspoons each cinnamon and allspice
1/2 teaspoon ginger
2 eggs
1/2 cup (80 g) currants
1/4 cup (50 g) diced candied lemon peel
3/4 cup (150 g) finely chopped dried figs
Grated rind of 1 lemon

Follow directions for making chocolate pfeffernüsse, combining honey, brown sugar, and butter in sauce pan. Combine flours in a bowl with baking powder, soda, salt, and spices. Add eggs to honey mixture and combine with flour mixture. Add fruits, and mix. Divide dough in half. Shape and bake as for chocolate pfeffernüsse, then cool on a rack.

Advent Calendar

1 cup plus generous 1 tablespoon (¼ pint) honey
1 cup (200 g) sugar
2 eggs
¼ teaspoon salt
¼ cup (50 g) finely diced candied lemon peel
¼ cup (50 g) finely diced candied orange peel
1 teaspoon ground cinnamon
½ teaspoon ground cloves
¼ teaspoon ground cardamom
6 cups (850 g) flour sifted with 6 teaspoons baking powder

For the icing decorations

5 cups (500 g) confectioners sugar
3 egg whites

For the St. Nicholas figure

3½ ounces (100 g) almond paste
¾ cup, generous (80 g), confectioners sugar

In addition

Food coloring, confectioners' gold shots (dragées)
Colored sugar sprinkles or nonpareils

Butter a 13 × 17-inch (33 × 43-cm) baking sheet.

Heat the honey and sugar in a saucepan until both are dissolved. Remove from the heat and continue to stir until the mixture is lukewarm.

Whisk the eggs with the salt.

Add the candied lemon and orange peels, eggs, spices, and flour to the honey mixture and knead together thoroughly.

Preheat the oven to 425°F. (220°C).

On a work surface sprinkled with flour, roll out the dough into a thin rectangle the size of the baking sheet. Place it on the baking sheet, pierce at close intervals with a knitting needle, and bake 20 minutes on the center shelf of the oven. If blisters appear in the dough, pierce again with the needle.

Let the dough cool 5 minutes, lift from the baking sheet with a spatula, and allow to cool thoroughly on a wooden board. With a knitting needle or thin-bladed knife, mark off a border of boxes running around the entire rectangle, 5 boxes across on each short side and 7 down on each long side; each box should be just over 2½ inches (6½ cm) wide and just under 2½ inches (6½ cm) high. Below the top row, outline a second row of boxes. An area of about 7⅞ × 10½ inches (20 × 24½ cm) will remain empty in the center.

For the icing, beat the confectioners sugar and egg whites with an electric hand beater set at lowest speed until a smooth, shiny mixture is produced. It must be thickish, so as not to run when piped in a ribbon; beat in more sugar if necessary. Color half of the mixture yellow with food coloring. From the other half, color 1 tablespoon green and 1 tablespoon red. Set aside in separate containers, covered with damp cloths.

Make a pastry cone from parchment paper; fill it with white icing mixture. First pipe a line all around the edge, then fill in the borders of all the marked boxes. Place gold shots at the points where lines intersect. Pipe the numbers 1 to 23 inside the boxes and decorate the inner borders with yellow icing mixture.

Knead the almond paste with the confectioners sugar. Color 3 small pieces of the mixture respectively brown, red, and pink; color the rest yellow and roll out all pieces about 1/16 to 1/8 (2 to 3 mm) thick. Sketch a St. Nicholas figure on cardboard and cut it out. With the help of the pattern, cut out the trunk and arms from yellow almond paste, the face from pink, the hat from red. Attach the pieces to the cake with a little of the icing mixture. Form the hands and the tree trunk from brown almond paste, the nose and mouth from red. The remaining details are added to St. Nicholas and the tree with the white and green icing mixtures, as shown in photograph. Outline the trimming of the coat hem, sleeves, collar, and hat with icing mixture and sprinkle with colored sugar sprinkles. Decorate the tree with gold shots. Pipe the number 24 in the empty space, using the white and red icing mixtures.

For a base, it is best to use firm cardboard wrapped in aluminum foil, or a sheet of plywood slightly bigger than the cake. Paste a border of baker's lace paper around the edge of the base and place the calendar on it.

13

Fruit Wedges

For about 160 cookies
2 cups plus 3 tablespoons (700 g) honey
⅔ cup (200 g) molasses
7-8 cups (1 kg) flour
1½ cups (200 g) raisins
1½ cups (200 g) dried currants
1 cup (200 g) diced candied orange peel
½ cup (100 g) diced candied lemon peel
1 heaping cup (150 g) chopped blanched almonds
3 teaspoons ground cinnamon
½ teaspoon each ground cardamom, cloves, and allspice
1 large pinch of mace
1 lightly heaped teaspoon (10 g) potassium carbonate or 4-5 teaspoons single-acting baking powder (see second note on page 10)
5 tablespoons milk
2 pounds 3 ounces (1 kg) good-quality semisweet chocolate or confectioners chocolate-flavored coating

Place the honey in a saucepan with the syrup, bring to the boil, and cool.

Sift the flour onto a pastry board and make a depression in the center. Add the dried fruits and spices, then pour in the honey solution and knead to form a smooth dough. It should be soft but workable.

Dissolve the potassium carbonate in the milk and knead vigorously into the dough; it should be very evenly distributed. Allow the dough to rest, covered, several hours.

Preheat the oven to 400°F. (200°C).

Cut the dough into 8 equal-sized pieces and shape them into cylinders about 16 inches (40 cm) long. Lay them on a lightly buttered baking sheet, leaving plenty of space in between, and bake about 20 minutes on the center shelf of the oven. Let the bars of dough cool and cut each one diagonally into 20 pieces (semi-pointed shapes; see photograph).

Temper the chocolate as described on page 43 and coat the cookies with it as follows: place them one at a time in the bowl of tempered chocolate, turn with a fork to submerge it on all sides, and tap several times on the rim of the bowl to allow as much as possible to run off. Place on parchment paper and decorate the tops with a fork by pressing the tines into the still soft chocolate and slowly drawing it sideways. Allow to harden completely before removing from the paper.

There is a second and simpler way of making these cookies, though they won't have the typical partly rounded upper surface. Roll out the dough on a work surface dusted with flour at least 9/16 inch (1½ cm) thick. The rectangle of dough is then placed on a lightly buttered baking sheet and pressed again with the rolling pin so as to be absolutely uniform in thickness. Pierce the rectangle of dough at very close intervals with a skewer or fork to keep the dough from producing blisters in baking. Let the dough rest 30 minutes, if possible, and preheat the oven to about 400°F. (200°C). Bake the rectangle of dough 20-25 minutes on the center shelf. Allow to cool about 5 minutes and then loosen from the baking sheet with a knife. Place on a wooden board (if available) and cover the top with aluminum foil to keep it from drying out. Next day (no sooner) cut it into strips 1⅓ inch (3½ cm) wide and cut these into the wedge shape (see photograph). Temper the chocolate as described on page 43 and coat the cookies with it. They are dipped into the chocolate one at a time and lifted out with a fork, tapped to drain off excess on the rim of the bowl, and then placed on a sheet of parchment paper. The top is decorated by pressing the fork into the still soft chocolate and slowly drawing it sideways; this produces the shallow raised marks. Remove the cookies from the paper only when the chocolate coating is completely hardened.

Chocolate Honey Cookies

For about 80 cookies
1 cup, scant (240 mL), honey
1¼ cups (250 g) sugar
6 ounces (175 g) semisweet chocolate
3½ cups (500 g) flour
4½ cups (250 g) coarsely ground unblanched almonds
½ cup (100 g) finely diced candied lemon peel
2 teaspoons ground cinnamon
½ teaspoon ground cardamom
¼ teaspoon each ground cloves, ginger, and allspice
3 eggs

In addition
1 pound 10 ounces (750 g) semisweet chocolate

Heat the honey, add the sugar and dissolve it, and allow to cool.

Chop the chocolate into bits and dissolve over hot water in a double boiler or bain-marie; add to the honey.

Sift the flour onto the work surface, make a depression in the center, and add the almonds, candied lemon peel, spices, and eggs. Add the honey mixture, then knead to form a not too soft dough and allow to rest overnight, wrapped in foil.

Preheat the oven to 375°F. (190°C).

Roll out the dough about ⅛ inch (½ cm) thick and cut into rectangles about 1½ × 2¼ inches (4½ × 6 cm). Place on baking sheet, leaving a little room between cookies, and bake on the center shelf of the oven about 12-15 minutes; they should not be too dark. They will be hard and brittle after baking and can be coated with tempered chocolate (see page 43). If kept in a well-sealed tin, they will become soft after about 8 days.

Honey Cakes

For 48 cookies
1½ cups (350 mL) honey
½ cup (125 mL) oil
1¼ cups (250 g) sugar
5 cups (700 g) flour
4 teaspoons baking powder
4½ cups (250 g) ground blanched almonds
2 teaspoons ground cinnamon
1 large pinch of ground cloves
½ teaspoon ground allspice
1 pinch of salt
3 eggs
½ cup (100 g) diced candied lemon peel
½ cup (100 g) diced candied orange peel
3 tablespoons evaporated milk

In addition
⅔ cup (100 g) blanched almonds
½ cup (100 g) diced candied lemon peel
⅔ cup (100 g) candied cherries

Bring the honey to the boil with the oil and sugar, stirring, and allow to cool again.

Sift the flour with the baking powder and combine with the almonds, all the spices, the eggs, candied lemon peel, and candied orange peel.

Add the honey-oil mixture to the flour mixture and knead thoroughly. If the dough is too soft, add more flour.

Let the dough rest in the refrigerator, covered, 60 minutes.

Oil a 13 × 17-inch (33 × 43-cm) baking pan. Preheat the oven to 400°F. (200°C).

Dusting your hands with flour, press the dough into the baking pan and smooth the surface; brush with the milk.

With a knife, lightly score the dough to mark off about 48 cookies. Decorate each cookie with almonds, pieces of candied lemon peel, and cherries.

Bake the honey cakes on the center shelf for 35-45 minutes. Let the cake cool slightly; remove from the pan and cut into bars as marked.

COOKIES MADE WITH BEATEN EGGS

Springerle

A Christmas cookie from Germany and Switzerland which is undergoing a real renaissance, in good part because of its marvellous traditional shape. The wooden molds are, in their own way, examples of a German folk art. This cookie is not only subtly flavored but the molds enable even novices to produce charming-looking cookies. Those with further artistic ambitions can paint the Springerle (see photo); in that case the water-based dough that follows the main recipe is recommended, since the cookies will no longer be suitable for eating.

For about 30-60 cookies, depending on the size of the molds
4 eggs
5 cups (500 g) powdered sugar
3½ cups (500 g) flour
Aniseed for sprinkling the baking sheet

Beat the eggs and powdered sugar in electric mixer or with electric hand beater until the sugar is completely dissolved and the mixture is light and airy. Work in the flour and let the dough rest, wrapped in foil, at least 1-2 hours.

Briefly knead the dough once more and place it between two wooden bars of ⅜-inch (1-cm) thickness. Dust the upper surface of the dough with flour or cornstarch and smooth with the balls of your thumbs. Press the mold into the dough, picture side down, and lift it straight up. The carved image must be visible down to the last detail. (Incidentally, in no case should the mold itself be sprinkled with flour or cornstarch, since this will cause the fine carved details to disappear in the course of time.)

Cut out the Springerle (using the molded borders as a guide) and allow to dry overnight on a baking sheet thinly dusted with flour.

Preheat the oven to 325°F. (160°C).

Coat a baking sheet very lightly with flour, sprinkle with aniseed, and place the Springerle on it. Bake for 20-30 minutes on the center shelf, with the oven door slightly ajar; cookies should be very light in color. The dried upper surface should remain as white as possible, but the lower part should rise to form a little "foot."

Variation:
Water-Based Dough

If Springerle are to be made only for decorative purposes (tree ornaments, for example), this water dough with its significantly shorter drying time is recommended. Mix 6¼ cups (625 g) powdered sugar with 1 cup (¼ L) lukewarm water until the sugar is dissolved. Work in 6¼ cups (900 g) flour. The dough should be stiff but not crumbly. It is then handled as in the preceding recipe.

Anise Cookies

An advantage of this beloved Christmas cookie is that if you have some familiarity with handling a pastry bag they are even easier to make.

For about 120 cookies
5 eggs
1½ cups (300 g) sugar
1 large pinch of salt
2¼ cups (300 g) flour
3 teaspoons aniseed

Place the eggs, sugar, and salt in a bowl. Choose a saucepan large enough to hold the bowl and fill it with just enough water not to overflow when the bowl is placed in it. Heat the water; place the bowl in the water bath and beat the egg-sugar mixture with a wire whisk until warm. It should reach about 105°F. (40°C). Remove the bowl from the water bath and beat the mixture slowly until cold.

With a wooden spatula, fold the flour and aniseed into the sugar mixture. Spoon this mixture into a pastry bag fitted with a plain tip.

Butter a baking sheet, dust it with flour, and pipe small dollops of batter onto the baking sheet at well-separated intervals. Let the anise cookies dry at least 10 hours or preferably overnight. They must have developed a dry upper surface and should be dry enough to be moved freely on the baking sheet.

Preheat the oven to 320°F. (160°C).

Bake the anise cookies on the center shelf 15 minutes. Since the upper surface of the cookies is dry, the dough can expand only underneath, producing the characteristic "feet."

Thorn Cookies

For about 40 cookies
1¾ cups (250 g) flour
1¼ cups (250 g) sugar
2 eggs
1 tablespoon aniseed
Grated rind of 1 lemon

Sift the flour into a bowl. Beat the sugar with the eggs until light and airy and fold in the flour a spoonful at a time. Fold in the aniseed and lemon rind.

Shape the dough into cylinders about the thickness of a finger, cut into pieces about 2-2⅓ inches (5-6 cm) long, and shape these into crescents. With a thin, sharp knife, score three oblique cuts in the upper side of the little crescents.

Place the cookies on a buttered and floured baking sheet and allow to rest overnight.

Preheat the oven to 375°F. (190°C). Bake the cookies 20-25 minutes on the center rack.

Meringue Tree Ornaments

Except for candles, you can dispense with other ornaments and trim an entire tree to marvellous effect with these light, airy decorations.

For 25-35 ornaments, depending on size
5 egg whites
2 cups (200 g) powdered sugar
Parchment or silicone paper, food coloring, cocoa, confectioners' gold or silver shots (dragées), chopped almonds or pistachios

Place the egg whites and powdered sugar in a clean bowl and beat lightly.

Choose a saucepan large enough to hold the bowl and fill it with just enough water not to overflow when the bowl is placed in it; heat the saucepan of water.

Place the bowl in the water bath and beat the egg white-sugar mixture. When the whites are stiff and warm to the touch (about 115°-120°F./45°-50°C), remove from the water bath and beat slowly until cooled. If an electric hand beater is used, it should be on medium speed.

The beaten egg white mixture can be put into a pastry bag and piped onto the sheet in any preferred shapes; choose a star tip or use a plain tip. The meringue mixture can also be tinted—for example, pink with red food coloring or brown with a little cocoa powder.

The piped shapes can also be sprinkled with different kinds of confectioners' shots (dragées) or chopped almonds or pistachios. You can also pipe small flowers or other shapes (especially successful with plain tip) and attach them together with imported nougat spread or melted chocolate.

Baking—more drying than baking, actually—is best done overnight at a temperature of 120°-140°F. (50°-60°C) or for 2-3 hours at 200°-210°F. (90°-100° C). The oven door *must* be kept open a crack to let moisture escape.

Variation: Macaroon Tree Ornaments

8¾ ounces (250 g) almond paste
¼ cup, generous (60 g), butter
⅓ cup, scant (30 g), powdered sugar
Grated rind of 1 lemon
3 egg yolks
9 ounces (250 g) semisweet chocolate
Parchment paper, chopped pistachios, confectioners' gold and silver shots (dragées)

Cut the almond paste into dice and knead half of it with the butter and sifted powdered sugar until evenly combined, then beat in the remaining almond paste, lemon rind, and egg yolks to produce a homogeneous but not frothy or over-aerated mixture.

Preheat the oven to 350°F. (170°C). Line a baking sheet with parchment paper.

Spoon the macaroon mixture into a pastry bag fitted with a star tip and pipe rings onto the baking sheet. Bake on the center shelf until golden brown, about 17 minutes. Let the macaroons cool and loosen from the paper.

Temper the chocolate as described on page 43. Dip the cooled macaroon rings into the chocolate, tap off excess on the rim of the bowl, and sprinkle with pistachios and gold and silver shots. Allow to dry on a cake rack.

SPICE COOKIES

Spekulatius

The home of this crisp Christmas cookie is in the Rhine area and neighboring Holland. The name can be derived from the Latin word *speculator* (overseer), as the function of a bishop was formerly defined. And, it is in honor of a bishop, St. Nicholas of Myra, that Spekulatius is said to have been created.

The many variations of Spekulatius have one thing in common. They are all made with an abundance of spices: cinnamon, cloves, and mace or nutmeg. Traditionally the dough is pressed into molds specially carved to make cookies with. But no one needs to forgo making Spekulatius for lack of the proper mold. The spicy dough can be rolled out and cut with cookie cutters instead.

For about 60 cookies, rolled and cut with a 2-inch (5-cm) cutter; or about 30 large or 80-90 small figures
½ cup plus 3 tablespoons (160 g) butter
2 cups (300 g) light brown sugar measured without packing
¼ teaspoon salt
1 cup (50 g) finely ground blanched almonds
1 egg
4 to 6 tablespoons milk
3 cups (400 g) all-purpose flour
1 teaspoon ground cinnamon
¼ teaspoon each cardamom, cloves, and mace
Milk

Cream butter and light brown sugar together. Beat in salt, ground almonds, egg, and 3 tablespoons milk. Add flour and spices and enough of remaining milk to form a stiff dough. You may need to knead the dough to work in all the flour. Refrigerate dough for 30 minutes.

If using Spekulatius or any other cookie molds, dust each with flour or cornstarch. Press enough dough firmly into each mold to pick-up pattern. Trim excess dough around edges of mold with knife. Molded cookies will be somewhat thick, about ¼ inch (¾ cm) or so. Unmold cookies onto greased baking sheets, leaving at least 1 inch (2½ cm) of space between each cookie. Brush cookies lightly with milk. Bake at 400°F. (200°C) for 10 to 12 minutes, or until lightly browned.

For cookie cutter cookies, roll dough ⅜ inch (1 cm) thick on lightly floured board. Cut into desired shapes and place on greased baking sheets, leaving 1 inch (2½ cm) of space between each cookie. Brush with milk and bake as previously directed. Cookie cutter cookies will bake a little faster because of their more uniform size and slightly thinner dough.

Whole-Wheat Spice Bars

For about 65-70 bars
⅔ cup (100 g) raisins
¼ cup (50 g) chopped dates
¼ cup (50 g) diced candied orange peel
½ cup (100 g) diced candied lemon peel
1½ jiggers (3 cL) rum
¾ cup plus 2 tablespoons (200 g) softened butter
½ cup, scant (125 mL), honey
2½ tablespoons (50 g) molasses
3 eggs
3½ cups (450 g) whole-wheat flour
4 teaspoons single-acting baking powder (see note)
½ cup, scant (40 g), cocoa
1½ teaspoons ground cinnamon
¼ teaspoon each ground allspice, cloves, and ginger
1 cup, heaping (150 g), coarsely chopped almonds
1¼ cups (150 g) coarsely chopped walnuts

For the icing
1 teaspoon egg white
2 teaspoons lemon juice
2 cups (200 g) powdered sugar

Place the dried fruits in a bowl, pour the rum over them, and allow to steep, covered, until soft—about 30 minutes.

Beat the butter with the honey and molasses until smooth but not frothy or over-aerated. Beat in the eggs one at a time.

Combine the flour with the baking powder, cocoa, and spices, add the almonds and walnuts, and add to the butter-egg mixture along with the dried fruits. Knead to form a smooth dough. Let it rest 2-3 hours, wrapped in foil.

Butter a baking sheet and sprinkle with flour. Preheat the oven to 400°F. (200°C).

Roll out the dough to a rectangle about 13 × 17 inches (32 × 22 cm) and place it on the baking sheet. Pierce it with a fork to keep it from forming blisters in baking. Bake on the center shelf 20-25 minutes; allow to cool.

Beat the egg white, lemon juice, and confectioners sugar to form a heavy icing mixture; ice the spice bars with this. Allow to dry overnight and cut into rectangles the next day.

Note: Single-acting baking powder is available from some mail order sources, or you can make your own by combining baking soda with a pinch of cream of tartar.

Variation: Chocolate Spice Bars

Make the spice bars according to the preceding recipe, then coat them with tempered chocolate (see page 43) and sprinkle them with chopped pistachios or other nuts. Because of the chocolate coating, they remain fresh for quite a long time.

Bitter Orange Cookies

For 80-85 cookies
4 eggs
1⅔ cups (250 g) light brown sugar, measured without packing
2 tablespoons orange juice
Grated rind of 1 orange
1¾ cups (250 g) whole-wheat flour

In a bowl set in a pan of hot water (or other double-boiler or bain-marie arrangement), beat the eggs, brown sugar, orange juice, and orange rind, preferably with a wire whisk; temperature of the mixture should be about 115°F. (45°C). Remove the bowl from the water bath, slowly beat the eggs until cooled, and stir in the flour.

Spoon the mixture into a pastry bag fitted with a plain tip and pipe small rounds, well separated from each other, onto a buttered and floured baking sheet. Allow to dry until the cookies are dry enough to be moved freely on the sheet.

Preheat the oven in 325°F. (170°C). Bake the cookies about 10-12 minutes; they should remain very light in color. The typical "foot" is produced as they rise.

Elise's Lebkuchen

For about 60 cookies
1¾ cups (350 g) sugar
5 eggs
2½ cups (350 g) unblanched almonds
¾ cup, roughly (100 g), flour
¼ cup (50 g) finely diced candied orange peel
¼ cup (50 g) finely diced candied lemon peel
2 teaspoons ground cinnamon
¼ teaspoon ground cardamom
1 large pinch each of ground cloves, allspice, and ginger
Round German baking wafers (oblaten), about 3 inches (8 cm) in diameter
Almond halves and candied lemon peel for decoration

For the glaze
1 cup (200 g) sugar
2 tablespoons lemon juice
4 tablespoons water

Using a wire whisk or electric hand beater, beat the sugar with the eggs until light and foamy in a large bowl set in or over hot water. The mixture should not become warmer than 115°F. (45°C).

Remove the bowl from the water bath and continue beating until the mixture is cool.

Grind the almonds fine, combine with the flour, candied orange and lemon peel, and spices, and stir into the egg-sugar mixture.

With a spoon, place about 1 tablespoon of the mixture on each baking wafer and spread it with a knife (repeatedly dipped in water); mixture should be more thinly spread toward the edge of the wafer. Garnish with almond halves and candied lemon peel.

Let the cookies dry overnight on a board or work slab.

Preheat the oven to 350°F. (180°C).

Bake the cookies 15-20 minutes on the center shelf. They should be crusty only on the upper surface; they must remain moist on the underside, since otherwise they dry out.

For the glaze, combine the sugar with lemon juice and water and bring to the boil. Lightly brush the still-hot cookies with the mixture.

Chocolate Lebkuchen

For about 70 cookies
1¾ cups (350 g) sugar
5 eggs
1 cup (150 g) flour
3 cups (300 g) ground hazelnuts
¼ cup, heaping (60 g), finely diced candied orange peel
⅔ cup (60 g) cocoa
2 teaspoons ground cinnamon
¼ teaspoon each ground cloves and allspice
Round German baking wafers (oblaten), about 3 inches (8 cm) in diameter
14 ounces (400 g) good-quality semisweet chocolate
Colored sugar sprinkles or nonpareils

The preparation is the same as for Elise's Lebkuchen. The dough is spread out in just the same way on the wafers and allowed to dry overnight in the same way. The cookies are also baked 15-20 minutes at 350°F. (180°C) and must be completely cooled before being covered with tempered chocolate (see page 43). Decorate with colored sugar sprinkles.

BUTTER COOKIES

Butter Thins

It is best to avoid overworking a short butter-based dough, since it will become greasy and brittle and will resist rolling out and further handling. For this reason, work the dough only as long as absolutely necessary.

For 30-50 cookies, depending on cookie-cutter size
1¼ cups (125 g) powdered sugar
1 cup plus scant 2 tablespoons (250 g) butter
1 egg yolk
1 large pinch of salt
Grated rind of 1 lemon
2¾ cups (375 g) flour

In addition
1 egg yolk for glaze
Crystal sugar, colored sugar sprinkles, or chopped pistachios for sprinkling over cookies

In a bowl, cream together the powdered sugar, butter, egg yolk, salt, and lemon rind. Add the flour and mix quickly to form a rich short dough. Form into a ball and let rest in the refrigerator, covered with foil, at least 2 hours.

Roll out the dough about ⅛-³⁄₁₆ inch (3-4 cm) thick on work surface lightly dusted with flour and cut into preferred shapes.

Preheat the oven to 375°F. (190°C).

Place the cookies on the baking sheet, leaving plenty of space in between; brush with the beaten egg yolk and sprinkle with colored sugar or chopped pistachios.

Bake on the center shelf until golden brown, about 8-10 minutes—but judge strictly by sight. If the oven heats unevenly, remove cookies with a spatula as they are done.

Nougat Crescents

Ingredients and preparation are as in the preceding recipe for Butter Thins.

⅔ cup (200 g) imported nougat spread
Powdered sugar for sifting over cookies

On work surface sprinkled with a little flour, roll out the dough to just under ⅛ inch (½ cm) thick. Cut out crescents, using a cookie cutter about 2 inches (5 cm) long, and bake until light brown.

Melt the nougat in a double boiler or bowl set over hot water and allow to cool.

Very gently rewarm the nougat to no more than 90°F. (32°C) and coat the undersides of the crescents. Attach in pairs, undersides touching. Allow to harden and sift powdered sugar over the tops.

Raspberry Stars

Ingredients and preparation are as in the preceding recipe for Butter Thins.

Seedless raspberry jam or jelly
Lemon juice
Raspberry eau de vie
Powdered sugar

Roll out the dough on work surface just under ⅛ inch (½ cm) thick and cut out stars about 1½-2 inches (4-5 cm) in diameter. Warm the raspberry jam and use it to attach the stars in pairs; lightly coat the upper surface as well. Mix a thin, transparent glaze from lemon juice, a little raspberry eau de vie, and powdered sugar and thinly brush the raspberry stars with it.

Black and White Cookies

For about 60 cookies
½ vanilla bean
1¼ cups plus 1 tablespoon (300 g) butter
1½ cups (150 g) powdered sugar
2¾ cups (375 g) flour
1 large pinch of salt
½ cup, scant (40 g), cocoa
1 egg yolk for glaze
2 tablespoons milk

Cut open the vanilla bean and scrape out the seeds with the tip of a knife. Discard pod and cream together vanilla seeds, butter, and powdered sugar. Stir in the flour and salt. Knead quickly into a smooth dough. Divide in half. Knead the cocoa into half the dough. Divide each half of dough in half again, so that you have 2 portions of both white and chocolate dough. Wrap separately in plastic wrap and chill for 1 hour. Remove 1 portion each of chocolate and white dough from refrigerator. Shape each in a rectangle of about 8 × 6 inches (20 × 15 cm) in size.

Photo 1: Roll one portion at a time to ⅜-inch (1-cm) thickness. To help you produce perfectly even results, use ⅜-inch (1-cm) thick strips of wood placed on either side of one portion of dough. After both portions of dough have been rolled to ⅜-inch (1-cm) thick, trim edges so that rectangles have clean, square edges.

Photo 2: Slice both rectangles into ⅜-inch (1-cm) thick strips.

Photo 3: To assemble the strips, lay 3 parallel to one another, alternating chocolate and white dough strips. Brush in between and on top with egg yolk which has been beaten with milk. Build second layer by placing white strip on top of chocolate and chocolate on top of white, until 3 strips are on top of the first layer. Brush in between and on top of strips in second layer with egg yolk mixture. Press strips lightly together with fingers, and smooth surface and sides similarly. Repeat until all strips are used.

Photo 4: Remove remaining 2 portions of dough from refrigerator. Roll each out to ⅛-inch (2-cm) thickness. Place a block of prepared strips on top of rolled dough, making sure to have 4 inches to one side of block. Brush portion of rolled dough that will cover block with egg mixture. Pick up and cover block of dough with rolled dough. Smooth with fingers. Repeat using remaining dough and prepared dough blocks. Leftover dough may be re-rolled. Wrap covered dough blocks in plastic wrap and refrigerate 1 hour.

Photo 5: Remove from refrigerator and cut with a sharp knife (serrated works well) into ¼-inch (4-mm) slices. Discard imperfect ends. Place 1½ inches (3 cm) apart on ungreased baking sheets.

Photo 6: Bake at 350° F. (180° C) for 10 to 14 minutes. Cookies should become firm (when cool), but not brown. The idea is to watch them carefully as they cook so the light portion stays light and offers the best contrast to the chocolate portion.

Arrack Pretzels

For about 60 pretzels
½ vanilla bean
¾ cup plus 2 tablespoons (200 g) butter
3 cups (300 g) powdered sugar
1 egg yolk
1 large pinch of salt
2¼ cups (300 g) flour
1 egg white
3 jiggers (6 cL) arrack or dark rum
2 teaspoons lemon juice

Cut open the vanilla bean and scrape out the pith with the tip of a knife.

In a bowl, cream the butter and 1 cup (100 g) of the powdered sugar to form a smooth mixture; add the egg yolk and salt, together with the vanilla pith. Mix in the flour. Let this rich short dough rest, covered, in the refrigerator about 1-2 hours.

Divide the dough into 3 parts. Roll out each part on floured work surface into a rope 16 inches (40 cm) long, cut into 20 even-sized pieces, and roll these into thin ropes about 10 inches (25 cm) long.

Preheat the oven to 350°F. (180°C).

Shape the ropes of dough into pretzels and attach the ends with a little egg white.

Place the pretzels on an un-buttered baking sheet and bake on the center shelf until golden brown, about 10-12 minutes. Combine the arrack or rum with the lemon juice and remaining powdered sugar and stir to make a fairly thin glaze. Dip the pretzels into the glaze and allow to dry on a cake rack.

Chocolate Pretzels

For about 60 pretzels
¾ cup plus 2 tablespoons (200 g) butter
1 cup (100 g) powdered sugar
1 egg yolk
1 jigger (2 cL) rum
1 large pinch of salt
1¾ cups (250 g) flour
¾ cup, scant (70 g), cocoa
1 pound (500 g) semisweet chocolate

The preparation of the dough is the same as for the preceding arrack pretzels. In this case the flour and cocoa powder are sifted together to distribute the cocoa evenly. The pretzels are shaped according to the same method and baked 10-12 minutes on the center shelf at 350°F. (180°C).

Temper the chocolate as described on page 43 and dip the cooled pretzels in it. Place on parchment paper and let the coating harden.

Pangani

A distinctively spiced Italian butter cookie.

For about 90 cookies
1 vanilla bean
1¼ cups plus 1 tablespoon (300 g) softened butter
2½ cups (350 g) light brown sugar, measured without packing
1 teaspoon ground cinnamon
1 large pinch each of ground cardamom and allspice
1 large pinch of salt
3 bitter almonds, ground, or ¼ teaspoon almond extract
1 egg
4-5 tablespoons milk
5½ cups (750 g) flour
10 ounces (300 g) semisweet chocolate

Cut open the vanilla bean and scrape out the pith; place it in a mixing bowl along with the butter. Add the sugar, cinnamon, cardamom, allspice, salt, and ground almonds to the butter and cream all these ingredients together to form a smooth mixture. Now work the egg and the milk into the dough; finally blend in the flour as quickly as possible.

Divide the finished dough into 3 equal-sized pieces and roll them out into 3 cylinders about 8 inches (20 cm) long. With the aid of a dull knife, press the sides into a square so that when cut they will produce rectangular slices. Wrap in plastic and let the bars of dough rests, preferably overnight but at least 2 hours. Line a baking sheet with parchment paper. Preheat the oven to 375°F. (190°C).

Cut each roll into 30 slices. Place on the baking sheet, spaced well apart, and bake on the center shelf of the oven until light brown, about 12-15 minutes. Remove the baking sheet and let the *pangani* cool.

Temper the chocolate as described on page 43. Dip the *pangani* from corner to corner on the diagonal, wipe off the underside on the rim of the bowl, and let the cookies dry on parchment paper.

Almond Crescents

For about 30 cookies
½ cup, generous (125 g), butter
⅔ cup (125 g) sugar
1 egg
1 lemon
1 large pinch of grated nutmeg
1 small pinch each of cinnamon and ground cloves
1 cup, scant (125 g), flour
1 cup (125 g) hazelnuts
2½ cups (125 g) fine bread crumbs, preferably homemade from good-quality Kaiser rolls
1 egg yolk for glaze
90 almond halves

Cream the butter with the sugar, then add the egg, grated rind of ¼ lemon, and the spices.

Sift the flour into a bowl.

Grind the hazelnuts. Add them to the flour along with the bread crumbs and quickly blend with the butter mixture to form a dough. Allow to rest in the refrigerator 2 hours, covered.

Dust the work surface very lightly with flour and roll out the dough on it 3/16 (½ cm) thick. If the dough sticks, loosen it from the work surface with a long cake cutter or spatula and dust a little flour under it again.

Preheat the oven to 375°F. (190°C).

Cut out into scalloped arcs (though of course any other shape will also be acceptable) and place on a very lightly buttered baking sheet.

Beat the egg yolk, brush the cookies with it, and top with 3 almond halves apiece. Bake the cookies on the center shelf until light brown, about 12-15 minutes.

S-Cookies

For about 40-50 cookies
1 cup plus scant 2 tablespoons (250 g) butter
1¼ cups (125 g) powdered sugar
1 large pinch of salt
Grated rind of ½ lemon
3 egg yolks
2¾ cups (400 g) flour

In addition
1 egg yolk for glaze
¼-⅓ cup (50-70 g) crystal sugar for sprinkling on cookies

In a bowl, cream the butter with the powdered sugar, salt, and lemon rind; add egg yolks and blend to form a creamy mixture. Sift the flour over this and quickly knead to form a rich short dough. Wrap in foil and allow to rest in the refrigerator at least 3-4 hours, preferably overnight.

Shape the dough into a roll and slice off equal-sized pieces. Roll them out into narrow ropes 3-3½ inches (8-9 cm) long and place on the unbuttered baking sheet, formed into S-shapes. Be sure there is enough space in between, since the cookies spread slightly.

Preheat the oven to 375°F. (190°C).

Beat the egg yolk with a few drops of water or milk. Brush the cookies with this and sprinkle with crystal sugar while the egg yolk is still wet. If any of it falls onto the baking sheet, remove it with a brush, since the sugar will scorch in baking.

Bake on the center shelf of the preheated oven until golden, about 10 minutes. Lift from the baking sheet with a spatula while still warm and allow to cool on a cake rack.

Orange Cats' Tongues

For about 30-35 cookies
3½ ounces (100 g) almond paste
¾ cup plus 1 tablespoon (200 g) butter
1 cup (100 g) powdered sugar
Grated rind of 2 oranges
4 egg yolks
1¾ cups (200 g) flour

In addition
⅔ cup, generous (200 g) orange marmalade
7 ounces (200 g) semisweet chocolate

Cut the almond paste into dice, combine in a bowl with the powdered sugar and half the butter, and beat until smooth. The almond paste must be completely incorporated with the other ingredients. Beat in the remaining butter, orange rind, and egg yolks. Sift the flour over the mixture and beat it in as well.

Butter a baking sheet and sprinkle with flour. Preheat the oven to 375°F. (190°C).

Spoon the dough into a pastry bag fitted with a plain tip and pipe strips in the shape of cats' tongue cookies (about 2-2⅓ inches/5-6 cm long) onto the baking sheet. Be sure there is plenty of space in between, since the dough will spread.

Bake the cookies on the center shelf 10-12 minutes; remove with a spatula while still hot. Spoon the marmalade into a paper cone. Pipe it onto the underside of the cookies and attach them in pairs.

Temper the chocolate as described on page 43 and dip the cookies halfway. Carefully wipe off the excess on the rim of the bowl and allow to harden on parchment paper.

Chocolate Nut Bars

This cookie is especially short-textured and "sandy."

For about 70 cookies
½ vanilla bean
¾ cup, generous (180 g), butter
1 cup (100 g) powdered sugar
1 egg
3 ounces (80 g) semisweet chocolate
2 cups (300 g) flour
1 cup (70 g) finely ground hazelnuts

In addition
7 ounces (200 g) semisweet chocolate
Chopped hazelnuts for scattering on cookies

Cut open the vanilla bean and scrape out the pith with the tip of a knife.

Cream the butter with the powdered sugar, vanilla pith, and egg to form a smooth but not frothy or over-aerated mixture.

Melt the chocolate in a double boiler or bain-marie arrangement and beat it into the butter mixture while still warm, then beat in the flour and very finely ground hazelnuts.

Preheat the oven to 375°F. (190°C).

Immediately fill the dough into a pastry bag and pipe onto a baking sheet in decorative shapes. Place on an unbuttered baking sheet, leaving plenty of space in between. Bake on the center shelf of the oven until golden brown, about 10-12 minutes, remove, and allow to cool.

Temper the chocolate as described on page 43 and dip the cookies a third of the way. Wipe off the excess on the rim of the bowl and place on parchment paper to harden. Sprinkle with chopped hazelnuts while the chocolate coating is still soft.

Curlicue Cookies

For about 80 cookies
1¼ cups plus 1 tablespoon (300 g) softened butter
2½ cups (250 g) powdered sugar
1 cup (125 g) cornstarch
¾ cup milk
Grated rind of ½ lemon
1 large pinch of salt
3½ cups (500 g) flour
Candied cherries or tempered chocolate

Cream the butter with the powdered sugar in a bowl until smoothly combined but not frothy or over-aerated. Beat in the cornstarch and ½ cup of the milk, along with the lemon rind and salt. Add the flour and knead to form a rich short dough. If the dough is very stiff, add the remaining milk.

Preheat the oven to 375°F. (190°C).

Pipe the dough out in decorative shapes, using a large nozzle. Garnish the cookies with candied cherry halves. Bake on the center shelf 12 minutes, until golden.

If they are to be coated with tempered chocolate, the cookies must be completely cooled first. Temper the chocolate as described on page 43 and dip the cookies a third of the way; wipe off the excess on the rim of the bowl and place on parchment paper to harden.

Tempering Chocolate

Christmas baking and chocolate go together, plain and simple. But *getting* them together is not so simple, as anyone knows who has ever dipped cookies into warm melted chocolate and waited in vain for it to harden . . . and if it finally *did* harden (maybe with the help of the refrigerator) it might have been gray and streaky instead of a lovely, glistening chocolate brown. Of course, the contrary caprices in the handling of chocolate coatings can be got round by replacing it with a confectioners' chocolate-flavored coating (bought ready to use). But this is a coating of vegetable fat and cocoa, which is very easy to work with but can't stand up to a comparison with real chocolate in terms of flavor. For this reason, I have always specified only real cooking chocolate in the recipes.

For coating cookies and cakes of superior quality, only genuine chocolate should be used; it is properly called *couverture,* from the French word meaning a coating. However, it cannot be used just as it is; in order to be satisfactory in terms of taste and appearance, it must first be "tempered."

What is the point of tempering? The chocolate you see—the *couverture*—consists of cacao, cocoa butter, and sugar. If the chocolate is to have fine flavor and the glazed cookie or cake is to have a nice brown sheen, the handling must be carried out at specific temperature—89°-90°F. (32°C). But (and this is the critical point) it is not enough simply to heat the chocolate to this temperature. This is only the first step. It must then be re-cooled until almost solidified, then warmed once more to 89°-90°F. This can be measured without a thermometer: a finger dipped in the coating ought still to feel cool.

Photo 1: Chop the chocolate into small bits with a sharp, heavy knife.

Photo 2: Place half the chocolate in a bowl and melt by setting the bowl over hot water, stirring constantly.

Photo 3: Scatter in the remaining chocolate and melt it in the already melted warm chocolate; this will also cool the melted chocolate. Let stand in the refrigerator until somewhat thickened and quite cooled.

Photo 4: Once more warm the chocolate slightly in the water bath until the tempered chocolate again becomes thin enough to flow freely.

Photo 5: Correct temperature can be tested with the help of a knife dipped in tempered chocolate: it ought to harden in a few minutes, and should have a satiny sheen and rich brown color.

Photo 6: Dip the cookies, then wipe off excess on the rim of the bowl. Place on parchment paper to harden. While you are doing this, it is best to leave the tempered chocolate in the water bath, so that it does not harden and require the repetition of the whole process all over again. Stir thoroughly from time to time to prevent any of the cocoa butter from separating.

Fruit-Nut Cookies

These cookies and the ones that follow are made with hazelnuts. In this recipe, the flavor of the nuts is most deliciously complemented by the fruit preserves. In the Hazelnut Dollars, spices underscore the typical aroma.

For about 60 cookies
1 vanilla bean
¾ cup plus 2 tablespoons (200 g) butter
½ cup (100 g) sugar
2 egg yolks
1 pinch of salt
2 cups (300 g) flour
1⅓ cups (100 g) ground hazelnuts
Powdered sugar to sift over cookies
⅔ cup (200 g) red currant jelly

Cut open the vanilla bean and scrape out the pith with the tip of a knife.

In a bowl, cream the butter with the sugar, then add the egg yolks, vanilla pith, and salt. Sift the flour over the mixture and work to form a rich short dough. Let the dough rest in the refrigerator 2 hours, wrapped in aluminum foil.

At this stage the dough will still be quite soft; carefully shape it into two cylinders each 12 inches (30 cm) long and chill these an additional hour.

Cut the rolls into slices ⅜ inch (1 cm) thick and shape them into balls. Place on an unbuttered baking sheet, leaving plenty of space in between, and make a depression in the center of each ball with the handle of a cooking spoon.

Preheat the oven to 400°F. (200°C).

Spoon the jelly into a pastry bag fitted with narrow plain tip and pipe it into the depressions. Bake the cookies about 12-15 minutes on the center shelf of the preheated oven. Sift powdered sugar over them.

Hazelnut Dollars

For about 60 cookies
1 vanilla bean
¾ cup plus 2 tablespoons (200 g) softened butter
1⅓ cups (200 g) light brown sugar, measured without packing
1 large pinch of salt
½ teaspoon each ground cloves and cinnamon
1 egg yolk
2 tablespoons milk
1⅓ cups (150 g) chopped hazelnuts
1¼ cups (200 g) flour
9 ounces (250 g) semisweet or couverture chocolate
¾ cup (80 g) chopped toasted hazelnuts to sprinkle on cookies

Cut open the vanilla bean and scrape out the pith with the tip of a knife.

Place the butter and brown sugar in a mixing bowl; add the salt and spices and cream the mixture with your hands. Work in the egg yolk and milk; finally mix in the chopped hazelnuts and flour. Divide the dough in half and shape into 2 cylinders each 8 inches (20 cm) long. Allow to firm up briefly in the refrigerator, then re-roll the cylinders to be sure they are perfectly round in cross-section, with no bulges or flattening.

Preheat the oven to 375°F. (190°C).

Let the rolls become thoroughly firm in the refrigerator (or leave 10 minutes in the freezer) and cut each into about 30 slices. Place on an unbuttered baking sheet, leaving plenty of room in between, and bake on the center shelf until a nice pale brown, 12-15 minutes.

Dip the cooled hazelnut dollars in the tempered chocolate (see page 43), wipe off the excess from the underside on the rim of the bowl, and place on parchment paper. Sprinkle with the chopped nuts.

Bread and Butter Cookies

For about 90 cookies
½ vanilla bean
¾ cup, generous (180 g), softened butter
1 cup (200 g) sugar
1 large pinch of salt
½ teaspoon ground cinnamon
1 egg yolk
3⅔ cups (200 g) ground almonds
4 ounces (110 g) semisweet chocolate, grated
1¾-2 cups (250 g) flour

For the icing
3 egg yolks
⅔ cup (75 g) powdered sugar
1 teaspoon lemon juice
Chopped pistachios for sprinkling on cookies

Cut open the vanilla bean and scrape out the pith with the tip of a knife.

On work surface, cream butter, sugar, seasonings, and egg yolk to form a creamy mixture. Combine the almonds and chocolate with the flour and quickly mix with the butter mixture. Divide the dough into 2 equal-sized pieces and roll into two cylinders each about 12 inches (30 cm) long. Place on a surface sprinkled with flour and press to flatten slightly. Allow to firm up in the refrigerator 2-3 hours (or overnight).

Preheat the oven to 375°F. (190°C).

Cut each bar into 45 slices. Place on an unbuttered baking sheet, leaving plenty of room in between (they spread quite a bit in baking), and bake on the center shelf of the oven until crisp and brown, about 10-12 minutes.

Beat the egg yolk with the powdered sugar and lemon juice until very light and spread the mixture over the cookies, on the underside (which looks more like a slice of bread). Sprinkle with chopped pistachios.

Milan Crescents

The foundation for these delightful cookies is always a short dough enriched with eggs.

For about 120-150 cookies, depending on cutter
1 cup, scant (250 g), softened butter
2½ cups (250 g) powdered sugar
1 large pinch salt
Grated rind of 1 lemon
3 eggs
3¾ cups (500 g) flour
2 egg yolks for glaze
Almond halves for topping (120-150 halves)

On work counter, cream together the butter, powdered sugar, salt, and lemon rind to form a creamy mixture. Gradually blend in the eggs. When they are thoroughly incorporated into the butter mixture, knead in the flour. Let the dough firm up 2-3 hours in the refrigerator.

Preheat the oven to 375°F. (190°C).

Roll out the dough about a scant ⅛ inch (3 mm) thick and cut out cookies with a crescent-shaped cutter (2-2½ inches/5-6 cm long). Place on an unbuttered baking sheet, brush with the beaten egg yolk, and top each with an almond half.

Bake on the center shelf of the oven until golden, about 10 minutes.

Almond Bars

For about 40 cookies
¾ cup plus 2 tablespoons (200 g) softened butter
⅔ cup (120 g) sugar
Grated rind of 1 lemon
1 egg yolk
3¼ cups (180 g) ground unblanched almonds
2 cups, roughly (270 g), flour
½ cup, scant (150 g), raspberry jam

For the icing
9 ounces (250 g) good-quality semisweet chocolate
45 almond halves
1 egg white and sugar (for sugar-coating the almonds)

Cream the butter with the sugar, lemon rind, and egg yolk; knead in the almonds and flour. Chill the dough overnight.

Preheat the oven to 350°F. (180°C).

Roll out the dough about ⅛ inch (3-4 mm) thick and cut into rectangles of 1⅔ × 1 inch (4½ × 2½ cm). Place on an unbuttered baking sheet and bake about 12 minutes on the center shelf.

Brush half of the bars with the warmed jam and sandwich together in pairs. Temper the chocolate as described on page 43 and dip the upper side of the cookies in the coating.

Dip the almonds first in the egg white, then the sugar and place on the still-soft coating.

Vanilla Crescents

For about 80 cookies
1 vanilla bean
⅔ cup, generous (100 g), blanched almonds
2 cups (280 g) flour
½ cup, scant (90 g), sugar
1 large pinch of salt
¾ cup plus 2 tablespoons (200 g) softened butter, cut into thin slivers
2 egg yolks
Vanilla sugar, made from ¾ cup (150 g) sugar and the pith of 1 vanilla bean

Cut open the vanilla bean and scrape out the pith. Grind the almonds very fine. With a large knife, using a chopping motion, blend together the almonds with the flour, sugar, salt, vanilla pith, and butter on a work slab. Add the egg yolk and knead to form a dough. Chill, wrapped in foil. Shape the dough into a cylinder and cut into 50 equal-sized pieces.

Preheat the oven to 375°F. (190°C).

Form the pieces of dough into small rolls with pointed tapering ends; shape these into crescents and place on an unbuttered baking sheet. Bake on the center shelf until light brown, about 12 minutes. Dredge the crescents in the vanilla sugar while still warm.

Walnut Hearts

For about 40 cookies
½ vanilla bean
½ cup plus 2 tablespoons (150 g) butter
1⅓ cups (130 g) powdered sugar
1 large pinch each of salt and ground ginger
1 egg yolk
1¾–2 cups (250 g) flour
1⅓ cups (60 g) ground walnuts
1¾ ounces (50 g) almond paste
⅓ cup, scant (100 g), orange marmalade

In addition
9 ounces (250 g) good-quality semisweet chocolate
Walnut halves for topping
Flour for dusting work surface

Cut open the vanilla bean and scrape out the pith with the tip of a knife.

In a bowl, cream the butter to a smooth and light consistency with the sugar, salt, ginger, and vanilla pith, then work in the egg yolk. Add the flour and walnuts and quickly knead to form a homogeneous short dough. Do not under any circumstances work it longer than necessary, since otherwise the dough becomes overshortened and brittle. Let the dough rest for 1-2 hours in the refrigerator, wrapped in foil.

Preheat the oven to 375°F. (190°C).

Roll out the dough a scant ⅛ inch (3 mm) thick on a work surface dusted with flour and cut out small hearts (about 2 inches/ 5 cm across). Place the cookies on an unbuttered baking sheet and bake on the center shelf of the oven until a nice light brown, about 10 minutes.

Cut the almond paste into small dice and beat until smooth with the orange marmalade. Use this orange-marzipan mixture to sandwich together the cookie hearts in pairs. Temper the chocolate as described on page 43. Dip the upper side of the cookie hearts into the coating and top each with a walnut half.

An especially nice variation is achieved by sandwiching together the hearts with warmed nougat spread instead of the orange-marzipan mixture.

Chocolate Hearts

For about 30 cookies
¾ cup plus 2 tablespoons (200 g) butter
⅔ cup (120 g) sugar
Grated rind of 1 lemon
1 egg yolk
3¼ cups (180 g) ground unblanched almonds
2 cups, roughly (270 g), flour

For the filling
⅓ cup (60 g) sugar
2 jiggers (4 cL) water
1 teaspoon lemon juice
1 jigger (2 cL) maraschino liqueur or other sweet cherry brandy
4¼ ounces (120 g) almond paste
9 ounces (250 g) good-quality semisweet chocolate
Pistachios for topping

Prepare a rich short dough by the method given in the recipe for Almond Bars on page 48; chill.

Preheat the oven to 350°F. (180°C).

Roll out the dough (this takes some patience) to about ¼ inch (¾ cm) and cut out hearts about 2½ inches (6 cm) across. Place on an unbuttered baking sheet and bake on the center shelf until light brown, about 12 minutes. Boil the sugar with the water and lemon juice for a few minutes until sugar is thoroughly dissolved. When cooled, combine with the maraschino liqueur and almonds to form a spreadable mixture. Sandwich the hearts together in pairs. Temper the chocolate as described on page 43; coat the hearts with it and sprinkle with finely chopped pistachios. (These cookies are shown in the photograph on page 49.)

Almond Sandies

For about 70 cookies
1/2 vanilla bean
2 ounces (60 g) almond paste
3/4 cup (200 g) butter
3/4 cup (80 g) powdered sugar
1/8 teaspoon salt
1 3/4 cups (250 g) flour
1 egg yolk, beaten
Sugar

Cut open vanilla bean and remove pith with tip of knife.

Cream together pith, almond paste, butter, and powdered sugar. Add salt and flour and form into a dough. Divide dough into 2 equal portions and shape each into an 11-inch (25-cm) long cylinder. Wrap in plastic wrap and refrigerate until firm, about 1 1/2 hours.

Preheat the oven to 375°F. (190°C).

Brush cylinders with egg yolk and roll in sugar. Slice each roll into about 35 rounds (each slice should be about 3/8 inch (3/4 cm) thick). Place on ungreased baking sheets and bake for 10 to 12 minutes, or until lightly browned.

Variation: Filled Sandies

For this, the cookies should be sliced somewhat thinner and baked for a shorter time, about 8-10 minutes. Heat 2/3 cup (200 g) imported nougat spread in a double boiler or bain-marie arrangement and thinly brush it over the flat underside of the cookies. The cookies are pressed together in pairs, undersides touching.

Danish Brown Cookies

These are called "brune kager" in Denmark, where they are the number one Christmas cookie— and deservedly so, given the exquisite flavor of these rich, spicy rounds. They are quick and easy to prepare. Generally speaking, the thinner they are sliced, the better; this can be done very simply and uniformly with a slicing machine—the sort used for cutting cold cuts.

For about 100 cookies
1 cup plus 2 tablespoons (250 g) butter
1 cup (200 g) sugar
1/2 cup (125 g) molasses
2 eggs
4 cups (500 g) all-purpose flour
1 teaspoon baking powder
1/4 teaspoon baking soda
2 teaspoons cinnamon
1/2 teaspoon each cloves and ginger
1/2 cup (75 g) finely chopped blanched almonds
1/3 cup (75 g) finely diced candied lemon peel

Combine butter, sugar, and molasses in heavy saucepan. Bring to boil over medium heat, stirring occasionally. Remove from heat and allow to cool. Beat in eggs. Stir in flour, baking powder, baking soda, cinnamon, cloves, ginger, almonds, and candied lemon peel. Cover dough with plastic wrap and allow to chill 1 hour. Remove from refrigerator and divide dough into 4 portions. Roll each portion into an 8-inch (20 cm) long cylinder. Wrap again and chill until firm. With a sharp knife or an automatic slicing machine, cut the cylinders of dough into very thin slices—1/8th inch (2 mm) is fine. Place 2 inches (5 cm) apart on greased baking sheets. Bake at 400°F. (200°C) for 7 to 10 minutes, or until beginning to turn brown. Allow to cool completely.

MACAROONS AND MARZIPAN COOKIES

Plain Macaroons

For about 150-200 macaroons, depending on size
1 pound (450 g) almond paste
1½ cups, scant (80 g), finely ground blanched almonds
2¼ cups (450 g) sugar
Grated rind of 1 lemon
6 egg whites (scant ¼ L)
Sugar for sprinkling over macaroons

Knead the almond paste together with the almonds, sugar, and lemon rind. Work in the egg whites with a wooden spatula, a little at a time; only when one addition is fully incorporated into the mixture is the next portion added.

Line baking sheets with parchment paper or silicone paper.

Spoon the mixture into a pastry bag fitted with a plain tip and pipe small, even-sized dollops onto the baking sheets. Sprinkle with sugar; remove excess sugar from the baking sheet with a brush. Let the macaroons dry for about 2 hours.

Preheat the oven to 310°F. (150°C). Bake the macaroons on the center shelf about 12 minutes. From the sprinkling of sugar, the macaroons should become especially crisp on top and also develop an attractive pattern of cracks over the upper surface.

Let the macaroons cool for about 5 minutes after baking and then invert the parchment paper so that the macaroons are underneath it. Brush the paper with cold water; after a few minutes the macaroons can be removed without difficulty.

Macaroon Caps

For about 40 cookies
1 pound (450 g) good-quality semisweet chocolate
½ cup (⅛ L) cream
3 tablespoons, scant (40 g), butter
1 jigger (2 cL) good rum
40 Plain Macaroons (see preceding recipe)
Crushed praline or other nut brittle for topping

Chop half the chocolate into small bits. Set other half pound aside. In a saucepan large enough to hold the above ingredients, scald the cream. Remove from the stove, immediately add the chopped chocolate, and stir with a whisk until it is completely dissolved. Place the hot cream mixture in the refrigerator and stir at intervals with the whisk to prevent a skin from forming on top. When the mixture is almost but not quite completely chilled, pour it into a bowl and whip until light and at least doubled in volume.

Cream the butter until very light (it must be of the same consistency as the cream mixture in order to combine with it easily) and stir it into the whipped mixture. Stir in the rum, a little at a time.

Cover the undersides of the macaroons with the mixture, making a peaked shape. Let them harden thoroughly in the refrigerator, then allow to warm up again at room temperature for about ½ hour. Temper the remaining chocolate as described on page 43, completely coat the macaroons with it, and sprinkle with the crushed praline.

Coconut Macaroons

For about 50 macaroons
3 egg whites
3 cups (300 g) powdered sugar
4 cups (300 g) flaked coconut
Small amount of cherry juice or red food coloring

Beat the egg whites with the powdered sugar until very light (electric mixer or electric hand beater is extremely helpful). Reserve ¼ cup of this egg white mixture and cover with foil.

Stir the flaked coconut into the remaining egg white mixture.

Line a baking sheet with parchment paper or silicone paper. With a teaspoon dipped in water, place small mounds of the mixture side by side; make a depression in the center of each with a cooking spoon handle.

Color the reserved egg white mixture pink with a little cherry juice or red food coloring; fill the hollows with this. The process is quite simple with a paper cone. Let the macaroons dry for about 2-3 hours.

Preheat the oven to 325°F. (160°C).

Bake the macaroons on the center shelf for 15-20 minutes; they should remain very pale. They should have a crinkly exterior but still be quite soft on the inside.

Fig Macaroons

For about 60 macaroons
3 egg whites
2½ cups (250 g) powdered sugar
⅔ cup, scant (120 g), chopped figs
½ cup (100 g) chopped dates
1⅛ cups (150 g) chopped almonds
Grated rind of 1 lemon
About 60 small round German baking wafers (oblaten)

Prepare the beaten egg white mixture as for Coconut Macaroons.

Fold the figs, dates, and almonds into the egg white mixture, along with the lemon rind. With a teaspoon dipped in water, place small dollops of the mixture on the baking wafers; set the wafers on baking sheets. Let the macaroons dry for about 2-3 hours.

Preheat the oven to 315°F. (160°C).

Bake the macaroons on the center shelf for about 10-15 minutes; these, like the Coconut Macaroons, should remain very pale, have a crinkly exterior, and be quite soft on the inside.

Walnut Macaroons

For about 45 macaroons
½ vanilla bean
3 egg whites
2 cups (200 g) powdered sugar
1⅔ cups chopped walnuts
About 45 small round German baking wafers (oblaten)
Walnut halves for garnish

Cut open the vanilla bean and scrape out the pith with the tip of a knife.

Beat the egg whites stiff, gradually trickling in about ⅔ of the powdered sugar. Gently fold in the remaining sugar, vanilla pith, and the chopped walnuts. With a teaspoon dipped in water, place small dollops of the mixture on the baking wafers. Top each with a walnut half. Let the macaroons dry about 2-3 hours.

Preheat the oven to 300°F. (150°C).

On the center shelf, bake the macaroons (actually, the process is heating to dry out rather than baking) for about 30 minutes. Like all macaroons, they should have a firm, crusty exterior and be soft on the inside. They are very delicate and fragile.

Rose-Hip Macaroons

These airy little macaroons are a typical Swabian specialty—hence the use of rose-hip jelly, popular in that region.

For about 100 macaroons
5 egg whites
5 cups (500 g) powdered sugar
Juice and grated rind of 1 lemon
⅓ cup (80 g) rose-hip jelly
11 cups, scant (600 g), ground blanched almonds

Beat the egg whites together with the powdered sugar until very light, preferably with electric hand beater. Reserve ½ cup of this mixture for filling and cover with foil. Using a wire whisk, beat into the remaining egg white mixture first the lemon juice and lemon rind, then the rose hip jelly and the ground almonds.

Line three baking sheets with silicone paper or parchment paper and place small, round macaroons on them, preferably using two teaspoons dipped in water to scoop out the macaroons.

Make a depression in the center of each and fill with the reserved egg white mixture, using a teaspoon or paper cone. Let the macaroons dry 2 hours.

Preheat the oven to 325° F. (160° C).

Bake the macaroons on the center shelf about 20 minutes.

Variation: Raspberry Foam Cookies

These are made exactly as for Rose-Hip Macaroons, except that the rose-hip jelly is replaced with a raspberry purée.

Simmer about ⅔ cup (100 g) fresh raspberries or about half of a 10-ounce (280-g) package of frozen raspberries with a generous ⅓ cup (80 g) sugar for about 8-10 minutes. Cool and force through a fine mesh sieve to remove the seeds. When completely cooled, it is folded into the macaroon mixture.

Pecan Macaroons

These macaroons can be made with walnuts instead, but only the original version yields such delicacy of flavor.

For about 100 macaroons
3½ ounces (100 g) dried figs
¼ cup (60 g) candied lemon peel
2 ounces (60 g) dates, pitted
1 jigger (2 cL) good dark rum
5 egg whites
5 cups (500 g) powdered sugar
Grated rind of 1 lemon
Grated rind of 1 orange
5¼ cups (500 g) freshly ground pecans
100 small round German baking wafers (oblaten)

Finely chop the figs, candied lemon peel, and dates; in a bowl, pour the rum over them. Let steep about 2 hours, well covered with foil.

In a bowl, beat the egg whites very light with the sifted powdered sugar.

Add the lemon and orange rind, the pecans, and the softened fruits; fold together all ingredients with a wooden spatula.

Place the baking wafers on baking sheets. With a coffee spoon dipped in water, place small dollops of the mixture on the wafers. Let the macaroons dry about 2 hours.

Preheat the oven to 310°F. (150°C).

Bake the macaroons on the center shelf for about 20 minutes; they should be no more than pale yellow.

Macaroon Bars

The batter for these macaroons is heated on top of the stove. In effect, the albumen in the egg white mixture coagulates slightly to thicken and bind it. It is simplest to beat the egg white in the same vessel that will then be used for heating the macaroon mixture.

For 60 macaroons
4 egg whites
1¼ cups (250 g) sugar
2⅔ cups (250 g) sliced almonds
Grated rind of 1 lemon
5 rectangular German baking wafers (oblaten), about 4¾ × 8 inches (12 × 20 cm)
9 ounces (250 g) good-quality semisweet chocolate

In a bowl entirely free of grease, beat the egg whites until just starting to stiffen and trickle in the sugar as you beat. The beaten mixture should have a just-pourable consistency. Stir in the almonds and grated lemon rind. Heat, stirring constantly (this is crucial, since the mixture sticks easily), until it is perceptibly thickened and feels hot. Distribute at once over the five baking wafers. Smooth the mixture with a knife dipped in water.

Preheat the oven to 325°F. (160°C).

Cut the filled wafers in half lengthwise (again, dip the knife in water first) and cut these strips into six pieces each. Place on a baking sheet and bake at 325°F. (160°C) for 18-20 minutes; they should remain pale. Allow to cool.

Temper the chocolate as described on page 43.

Dip the macaroon bars halfway in the chocolate coating. Carefully wipe off the excess from the underside on the rim of the bowl and place the bars on parchment paper.

Egg Yolk Macaroons

For 35-40 macaroons
8¾ ounces (250 g) almond paste
¼ cup, generous (60 g), butter
⅓ cup, scant (30 g), powdered sugar
Grated rind of 1 lemon
3 egg yolks
Candied cherries and almonds for garnish

Work half of the almond paste with the butter and powdered sugar until the butter is completely incorporated into the almond paste. Then beat in the remaining almond paste, lemon rind, and egg yolks. The mixture must become smooth, but not frothy or over-aerated.

Preheat the oven to 340°F. (170°C).

Spoon the mixture into a pastry bag fitted with a star tip and pipe in any preferred shapes on a baking sheet lined with parchment paper or silicone paper. Garnish with the candied cherries and almonds.

Bake on the center shelf of the oven until a nice golden color (about 15 minutes). Allow to cool; loosen from the paper. (If they stick, invert with the paper on top and brush with water. After a few minutes the macaroons will come free without effort.)

Cinnamon Stars

Ground almonds quickly turn rancid, so grind the almonds freshly yourself if at all possible.

For 60-80 cookies
6 egg whites
5 cups (500 g) powdered sugar
9 cups (500 g) ground unblanched almonds
2-3 teaspoons ground cinnamon
About 3⅔ cups (200 g) ground almonds for sprinkling on work surface

Combine the egg whites with the powdered sugar. Beat the mixture in a bowl to a very stiff consistency. An electric hand beater should be used for this—or, better yet, an electric mixer, since the beating is a weary and grueling task.

Remove a generous ½ cup of the well-beaten mixture and set it aside to be used for topping.

Place the ground almonds on a work slab. Combine with the cinnamon; work together with the egg white mixture to form a soft dough.

Lightly sprinkle the work surface with ground almonds and roll out the dough evenly about ⅜ inch (1 cm) thick. Spread the top with the reserved egg white mixture.

The cinnamon stars are now cut out with a star-shaped cookie cutter. To prevent the topping from sticking to the cutter, dip it repeatedly in cold water, using your fingers to help loosen if necessary. Place the cinnamon stars on a buttered baking sheet.

Knead together the leftover scraps of dough. Since the dough will become slightly softer from the egg white topping mixture, add some ground almonds. Once more roll out the dough in the same way, again spread with the egg white mixture, and so forth. If possible, let the cinnamon stars dry overnight.

Preheat the oven to 325°F. (160°C).

Bake the cinnamon stars on the center shelf; they should be very pale, and the top should remain white. This will take at most 7-8 minutes, depending on your oven. They should be firm on the outside but still soft on the inside.

Chocolate Spice Cookies

This Christmas cookie from Switzerland (its chief home territory is Basel) is directly related to the Cinnamon Stars. It can be cut out in any desired shape, though hearts are generally preferred.

For about 50 cookies
2 egg whites
1 tablespoon water
¼ cup (50 g) sugar
4½ cups (250 g) ground unblanched almonds
1 cup (200 g) sugar
4 ounces (100 g) unsweetened chocolate
1 large pinch of ground cinnamon
Sugar for rolling out the cookies

With wire whisk or electric hand beater, beat the egg whites with the water and sugar until just starting to stiffen.

Grate the chocolate. In a bowl, combine the almonds with the sugar, chocolate, and cinnamon. Add the egg white mixture and work it into these ingredients.

Sprinkle the work surface with sugar, place the dough on it, and roll out about ⅜ inch (1 cm) thick. Cut out hearts and place them on a buttered baking sheet. Allow to dry about 5-6 hours, or better yet, overnight.

Preheat the oven to 325°F. (160°C).

Bake the cookies on the center shelf 15 minutes. Like the Cinnamon Stars, they should be crisp on the outside but remain quite soft on the inside.

Bear Claws

Why these are called "bear claws" but actually made in scallop-shaped molds is not known, but this is a cookie with a real tradition. Those who don't have the appropriate molds can shape the dough into small balls, or roll it out and cut into any desired shape.

For about 60 cookies
3 egg whites
1¼ cups, scant (220 g), sugar
7 ounces (200 g) good-quality semisweet chocolate, grated
4½ cups (250 g) ground unblanched almonds
Grated rind of 1 lemon
½ teaspoon ground cinnamon
Sugar for sprinkling the mold

Beat the egg whites stiff, gradually trickling in ⅔ of the sugar.

Combine the remaining sugar with the grated chocolate, ground almonds, lemon rind, and cinnamon; fold into the egg whites. With a teaspoon, scoop out small dollops of the mixture (adjust amount by testing with the mold) and roll between your hands into balls. Sprinkle the mold with sugar, press each ball of dough into the mold, then turn it out again, knocking the edge of the mold against the work surface.

Butter a baking sheet and dust it with flour. Place the Bear Claws on it and allow to dry overnight.

Preheat the oven to 350°F. (180°C).

Bake the Bear Claws on the center shelf about 15 minutes. They should have a crisp outer crust but remain soft on the inside.

Hazelnut Meringue Sandwiches

For about 40 cookies
5 egg whites
1 cup (180 g) sugar
2 cups (250 g) shelled hazelnuts
⅓ cup (50 g) flour
¾ cup, generous (80 g), powdered sugar
½ cup (150 g) imported nougat spread for sandwiching together the meringue halves

Beat the egg white stiff, gradually trickling in the sugar.

Toast the hazelnuts either in a skillet on top of the stove or on a baking sheet in the oven. Let cool slightly to let the skins split, then rub between your hands to remove the skins completely. Grind the nuts fine and combine with the flour and powdered sugar. Fold into the egg whites with a wooden spatula.

Butter a baking sheet and dust it with flour.

Spoon the mixture into a pastry bag fitted with a plain tip and pipe small flat rounds onto the baking sheet. Place on the center shelf of the oven at 250°F. (120°C); they should dry out rather than bake. In about 2-3 hours they will be properly done: crisp on the outside and nice and soft on the inside.

Place the nougat spread in a small bowl or saucepan and heat to dissolve in a hot water bath. Let cool again and sandwich the meringue rounds together, undersides touching.

Iced Marzipan Cakes

For about 40 cakes
7 ounces (200 g) almond paste
1 cup (100 g) powdered sugar
2 cups, scant (100 g), ground blanched almonds
1 jigger (2 cL) rum
1 large pinch of salt
1 egg white for glaze
Almond halves

For the icing
1 cup (100 g) powdered sugar
½ jigger (1 cL) rum
1 jigger (2 cL) hot water

Cut the almond paste into dice. On work surface, knead to a smooth dough with the powdered sugar, finely ground almonds, rum, and salt. Divide the dough in half. Roll into two narrow cylinders each about 16 inches (40 centimeters) long; divide each into 20 pieces. Cover with a damp cloth to keep them from drying out.

One at a time, roll the pieces into balls, pinching each upwards to make a slightly pointed top.

Prehat the oven to 475°F. (250°C).

Beat the egg white slightly and thinly brush over the marzipan balls. Decorate each with three almond halves pressed against the sides.

Line a baking sheet with parchment paper or silicone paper, place the marzipan cakes on it, and quickly brown on the center shelf of the oven; keep an eye on them to keep them from becoming too dark.

Mix the powdered sugar with the rum and water and brush the still-hot cakes with the mixture. Allow to dry before storing in a container.

Marzipan Loaves

The recipe for these is very simple. Almond paste is thoroughly combined with powdered sugar in a ratio of two parts almond paste (best measured by weight) to one part powdered sugar. Great care must be taken with one essential: all equipment that comes into contact with the almond paste and sugar must be kept most scrupulously clean, since otherwise the marzipan will begin to spoil if stored for an extended period.

Sift the powdered sugar onto a *clean* work surface, cut the almond paste into dice, and knead to a smooth mixture together with the powdered sugar, in one smooth operation. Do not work the mixture too long, since the marzipan may become too greasy to be handled (the almond oil will separate from the solid matter).

For the loaves, weigh out pieces of about 1 ounce (30 g) apiece, roll them into evenly rounded balls, and form into slightly elongated loaf shapes. Score with a knife. The loaves can now be browned in a hot oven like the Iced Marzipan Cakes or allowed to dry overnight and coated with tempered chocolate (as described on page 43).

Marzipan Potatoes

Make almond paste mixture in a 2 : 1 ratio (see preceding recipe); shape into a long roll and cut into equal-sized pieces. Roll these into balls and immediately roll in cocoa. Tap off excess cocoa and score the potatoes with a knife to suggest split potato skins.

COOKIES MADE WITH FRUIT

Raspberry Rings

For about 30-35 cookies
3 cups (400 g) flour
⅔ cup (120 g) sugar
1 pinch of salt
Grated rind of 1 lemon
1 tablespoon vanilla sugar
1 egg yolk
1 jigger (2 cL) rum
1 cup plus scant 2 tablespoons (250 g) butter

For dusting and topping
2 tablespoons powdered sugar
¾ cup (250 g) raspberry jam

Sift the flour onto a pastry board. Make a depression in the center and add sugar, salt, lemon rind, vanilla sugar, egg yolk, and rum. Cut the butter into very thin slivers and distribute over the edges of the flour. Knead all these ingredients together to form a rich short dough. Let the dough rest in the refrigerator 2 hours, wrapped in aluminum foil.

Preheat the oven to 350°F. (180°C).

Working with a portion of the dough at a time, roll it out a scant ⅛ inch (3 mm) thick. Cut out equal numbers of rings and solid circles of identical diameter (2½ inches/6 cm). Place on an unbuttered baking sheet.

Bake on the center shelf 10-15 minutes. Lift the cookies from the baking sheet with a spatula and allow to cool on a cake rack.

Sift the powdered sugar over the rings. Stir the jam until smoothly melted over low heat, then brush the whole circles with jam and place the rings on top. Place a little more jam in the center. Allow to dry thoroughly.

Variation: Glazed Raspberry Rings

The dough for Raspberry Rings can be used for this cookie, but these are cut out with plain round cutters and sandwiched together in the same way with raspberry jam.

Mix dark rum with powdered sugar to form a thin, translucent glaze and thinly brush this over the sandwiched cookies. If they are to be stored on top of each other, they must be completely dry beforehand.

Linzer Wreaths

For about 50 cookies
4 hard-boiled egg yolks
1¼ cups, scant (120 g), powdered sugar
¾ cup plus 2 tablespoons (200 g) softened butter
2 tablespoons vanilla sugar
1 pinch of salt
2¼ cups (300 g) flour
1 cup (120 g) unblanched almonds
1 egg yolk
¼ cup red currant jelly

Force the hard-boiled egg yolks through a fine-mesh sieve and beat until light and airy with ¾ cup (80 g) sifted powdered sugar and the butter. Add the vanilla sugar, salt, and sifted flour and thoroughly knead all these ingredients together. Let the dough rest 2 hours in the refrigerator, wrapped in aluminum foil.

Pour boiling water over the almonds, let them steep briefly, rinse under cold water, slip off the skins, and chop coarsely.

Preheat the oven to 400°F. (200°C).

Roll out the dough about 3⁄16 inch (4 mm) thick and cut out rings about 2¾ inches (6 cm) in outer diameter and 1 inch (2½ cm) in inner diameter.

Beat the raw egg yolk, brush the rings with it on one side only, and press the glazed side into the coarsely chopped almonds. Place the rings on an unbuttered baking sheet, almond side up, and bake on the center shelf 10-15 minutes. Let the cookies cool.

Brush the underside of the cookies with the currant jelly (whisked until smooth) and sandwich the rings together in pairs.

Orange Cookies

For about 70 cookies
½ cup, generous (125 g), softened butter

⅞ cup (125 g), light brown sugar

4 ounces (100 g) good-quality semisweet chocolate

1 egg

1 large pinch of salt

Grated rind of 2 oranges

1⅓-1½ cups (200 g) flour

1 cup (100 g) powdered sugar

2-3 tablespoons orange juice

On a work slab, cream the butter with the sugar and finely grated chocolate. Add the egg, salt, and grated rind of 1 orange, then sift the flour over the mixture. Quickly knead to a smooth short dough and let it rest in the refrigerator, covered with aluminum foil, about 2 hours.

Roll out the dough about ⅛ inch (4 mm) thick.

Preheat the oven to 400°F. (200°C).

Cut out cookies about 2 inches (5 cm) in diameter, with crinkled edges, and place on an unbuttered baking sheet, leaving space in between (the cookies will spread a bit in baking). Bake on the center shelf until brown and crisp, about 8-10 minutes. Remove cookies from the baking sheet while still warm and allow to cool.

Beat the powdered sugar with the orange juice to form a thin icing mixture. Ice the top of the cookies and sprinkle with the remaining orange rind.

Whole-Wheat Citrus Spice Cookies

For about 80 squares
½ cup (100 g) diced candied lemon peel

⅓ cup (80 g) diced candied orange peel

½ cup (80 g) currants

1 jigger (2 cL) rum

1 cup (100 g) honey

⅓ cup (100 g) molasses

2 eggs

3 cups (200 g) ground blanched almonds

2½ cups (350 g) whole-wheat flour

1 teaspoon baking powder

¼ teaspoon baking soda

1 teaspoon cinnamon

¼ teaspoon each allspice and ginger

⅛ teaspoon each cloves and mace

1½ cups (200 g) chopped unblanched almonds

For the icing
1½ cups (100 g) powdered sugar

6 to 8 tablespoons lemon juice

In small nonmetal bowl, combine candied lemon peel, candied orange peel, currants, and rum. Stir to distribute rum. Cover and let stand at room temperature for 1 hour. Combine honey and molasses in heavy saucepan. Bring to boil, stirring occasionally. Remove from heat and allow to cool. Beat in eggs. Stir in ground almonds, whole-wheat flour, baking powder, baking soda, cinnamon, allspice, ginger, cloves, mace, and chopped almonds. Stir or knead into a rather tacky dough. Grease and flour a 13 × 17-inch (33 × 43 cm) baking pan (sides should be at least 1 inch (2½ cm) high), or 2 baking pans, each 9 × 13 inches (23 × 33 cm) in size. Lightly oil hands and pat dough into pan. Bake at 400°F. (200°C) for about 20 minutes, or until lightly browned. Remove from oven and let cool. Prepare icing by combining powdered sugar and enough lemon juice to make an icing of drizzling consistency. Drizzle evenly over baked, uncut cookies. Let stand at room temperature, uncovered until icing dries. When dry, cover tightly with plastic wrap or foil and store, unrefrigerated, for 1 to 2 days. Cut into 1 × 2-inch (2½ × 5-cm) bars.

Whole-Wheat Orange Thins

For about 80 cookies
1 cup plus scant 2 tablespoons (250 g) butter
1¾ cups (250 g) light brown sugar
2 eggs
½ teaspoon salt
Grated rind of 2 oranges
1 cup (150 g) whole-wheat flour
1 cup (150 g) white flour

On work surface, knead together the butter and sugar until soft and creamy. Work in the eggs, one at a time, then the salt and orange rind. Finally knead in both kinds of flour.

Shape the dough into two cylinders each about 14 inches (35 cm) long. Let them firm up somewhat in the refrigerator, then remove and reroll to be sure they are perfectly circular in cross-section, with no bulges or flattening. Again allow to become firm in the refrigerator.

Preheat the oven to 400°F. (200°C).

Cut the rolls into 40 slices each. Place on an unbuttered baking sheet, leaving plenty of room in between, and bake on the center shelf of the oven until crisp and light brown, 8-10 minutes.

Apricot Dollars

For 70-80 cookies
1 cup plus scant 2 tablespoons (250 g) butter
1⅓ cups (200 g) light brown sugar
¼ teaspoon each salt and ground ginger
Grated rind of 1 lemon
1 cup (200 g) flour
1¾ cups (150 g) rolled oats
1 cup, scant (100 g), apricot preserves

Beat the butter to a creamy consistency with the sugar, salt, ginger, and lemon rind. Add the flour and rolled oats and knead to form a homogeneous short dough. Shape it into two cylinders about 1 foot (30 cm) long and allow to firm up in the refrigerator. If necessary, reroll after an interval to be sure that the cylinders of dough are perfectly rounded in cross-section, with no bulges or flattening.

Preheat the oven to 400 °F. (200°C).

After another resting period, cut each cylinder into about 35 slices. Place them on an unbuttered baking sheet, leaving plenty of room in between, since they spread somewhat in baking. With a teaspoon, place a small dollop of apricot preserves on each and bake the cookies on the center shelf until crisp and brown, 8-10 minutes.

Variation: Raspberry Dollars

These are as crisp as Apricot Dollars, but spicier in flavor—the result of 1 teaspoon ground cinnamon, 1 large pinch ground cloves, and ¼ teaspoon ground allspice kneaded into the dough. The apricot preserves are replaced by raspberry jam. The preparation is the same as for Apricot Dollars; the baking time is again 8-10 minutes per baking sheet.

HOLIDAY BREADS/SPECIALTIES

Braided Fruit Bread

This is a braided loaf for the Christmas holiday, but it is also baked through the entire year. The characteristic shape is achieved by placing three separate yeast braids on top of each other. The first is a flat four-strand plait. A three-strand braid is laid over it, and on top a rope of two intertwined strands.

For one loaf
4½ cups (600 g) flour
1 package active dry yeast
1 cup (¼ L) milk
½ cup plus 1 tablespoon (130 g) butter
½ cup, scant (90 g), sugar
½ teaspoon salt
Grated rind of 1 lemon
1 egg
1 heaping cup (80 g) raisins
¼ cup, scant (40 g), diced candied lemon peel
¼ cup, scant (40 g), diced candied orange peel
1 egg yolk for glaze

Sift the flour into a bowl and make a hollow in the center. Sprinkle in the yeast and dissolve it in the lukewarm milk. Sprinkle a little flour over the yeast-milk mixture and let stand in a warm place about 15 minutes, until fissures are clearly visible on the surface.

Melt the butter and combine with the sugar, salt, lemon rind, and egg. Add this mixture, at luke-warm temperature, to the fermenting yeast-milk solution and beat all these ingredients together to form a smooth, firm yeast dough. Let rise 15 minutes, covered.

Work in the raisins, candied lemon peel, and candied orange peel and let rise another 15 minutes.

Divide the dough into nine portions, then shape each into balls, and roll into even-sized ropes about 27 inches (70 cm) long. Make one 4-strand braid, one 3-strand braid, and one 2-strand braid.

First, flatten the 4-strand braid and place on a lightly buttered baking sheet. Press to flatten somewhat with the edge of your palm, to make enough room to accommodate the succeeding 3-strand braid. Twine a rope from the last two strands and use egg yolk to secure it over the 3-strand braid. Let the braid rise thoroughly in a warm place, covered with a cloth. It should increase markedly in volume.

Preheat the oven to 400° F. (210° C).

Brush the braid with egg yolk and bake about 35-45 minutes on the bottom rack of the oven. If not sure, test with a wooden pick to be sure the dough is baked all the way through; no dough should cling to the surface. Sift powdered sugar over the cooled bread; or, if it has to remain moist for a long time, brush with warmed apricot preserves and a rum glaze.

For the rum glaze, 1 jigger (2 cL) dark rum is mixed with the same amount of powdered sugar (add carefully, a little at a time), until the glaze is milky but still somewhat transparent.

Christmas Stollen

This recipe is the version used in Dresden, the home of Christmas Stollen. Because of the high butter content, the butter cannot be kneaded in in a melted state as is usually done with yeast doughs; instead, it is softened and mixed with a small amount of flour.

For 2 Stollen
1 vanilla bean
7-8 cups (1 kg) flour
2 packages active dry yeast
1⅔ cups (¼ L) lukewarm milk
½ cup (100 g) sugar
2 eggs
Grated rind of 1 lemon
1 teaspoon salt
1¾ cups (400 g) softened butter
1½ cups, roughly (200 g), flour
2⅓ cups, generous (350 g), raisins
¾ cup (100 g) chopped blanched almonds
¼ cup (50 g) diced candied lemon peel
½ cup (100 g) diced candied orange peel
1-3 jiggers (2-6 cL) rum
½ cup plus 2 tablespoons, generous (150 g), butter for brushing on loaves
Vanilla sugar for dredging loaves, made from 1 cup (200 g) sugar and pith of 1 vanilla bean

Cut open the vanilla bean and scrape out the pith with the tip of a knife.

Sift the flour into a bowl. Make a depression in the center, sprinkle in the yeast, and dissolve it in the lukewarm milk. Sprinkle a little flour over the yeast-milk mixture and let stand 20 minutes, covered.

Add the sugar, eggs, vanilla pith, lemon rind, and salt to the fermenting yeast-milk solution and beat to form a firm dry dough. Let the dough rise 10-15 minutes.

Meanwhile, knead together the butter and flour to form a soft dough. Work this into the risen yeast dough. Let the dough rise once more for 15 minutes.

Combine the raisins, almonds, candied lemon peel, and candied orange peel. Pour the rum over them and let steep a while.

Quickly work the fruit mixture into the yeast dough and let the dough rise again 10-15 minutes.

Shape the dough into two balls and roll them into narrow rectangles about 12 inches (30 cm) long. With a rolling pin, flatten the rectangles in the center so as to produce fairly thick raised borders on the long sides. On the short ends, tuck in the dough somewhat to even the edges, then fold lengthwise into the well-known Stollen shape (see pages 78-79).

Line a baking sheet with buttered parchment paper, place the Stollen on it, and let rise 20-30 minutes, covered with a cloth.

They should increase markedly in volume.

Preheat the oven to 400°F. (200°C).

Bake the Stollen about 60 minutes on the bottom shelf of the oven and test with a wooden pick to be sure the dough is baked all the way through; no dough should cling to the surface.

Melt the butter; brush the still-warm Stollen with it on all sides and sprinkle with vanilla sugar. The coating of butter and sugar preserves the succulent fresh texture of the Stollen and helps prevent them from drying out.

Shaping a Stollen

The consistency of the dough is a crucial point for the success of a Christmas Stollen. The dough should be dry, but light and airy. After the butter is worked into the preliminary yeast sponge, another fairly long fermentation should follow, during which the dough should rise very emphatically.

The dough for Stollen doesn't really always have to be given the traditional shape. It is possible to allow free rein to one's fancy in shaping it—*but* it is not possible to turn the dough out into a rectangular bread pan (it rises too much and would spill over the edges) and it is not possible to put it into a tall, high-sided pan (the heavy dough will stay unbaked in the middle). There are still other reasons for the shape everyone is familiar with. Since the dough—which is very rich in fat and very heavy because of the large amount of dried fruit—tends to spread in baking, it cannot be made into a round shape, but only into flat loaves. For this reason, the long-familiar Stollen shape is the one that makes the most sense. How to achieve it is described in exact detail below. It's really not difficult.

Photo 1: When the dough has risen, place it on the work surface, pulling to spread it out slightly.

Add the dried fruits and/or nuts (the version in the pictures is an almond Stollen) and knead them in as quickly as possible. In Stollen with a high content of raisins or currants, this must be done with special care and dispatch to prevent the fruit from giving the dough an unappetizing gray color. After this step, let the dough rise once more, covered.

Photo 2: Roll up the dough into a ball and form this into a longish loaf shape. With a rolling pin, press to thin only the center of the dough. A thick raised edge must remain on both long sides.

Photo 3: To keep the Stollen uniform in width throughout the whole length, the rounded short ends of the dough must be folded toward the center and rolled with the rolling pin to incorporate them firmly. Stollen often have a filling added (for example, Christmas Stollen). This is done as follows: A long cylinder about ¾ inch (2 cm) thick is shaped out of almond paste and placed in the center of the Stollen. The bread is then given its final shaping as described below.

Photo 4: Fold the dough lengthwise so that the two raised borders lie side by side.

Photo 5: After baking, thoroughly brush the still-warm Stollen with hot melted butter; even the underside of the Stollen should be uniformly coated.

Photo 6: Sugar is very thoroughly combined with the pith of a vanilla bean. Spread out a portion of the sugar on parchment paper. Place the buttered Stollen on it, very carefully—the still-warm Stollen is extremely fragile. Dredge on all sides with the remaining vanilla sugar. The Stollen should rest at least a week, covered with aluminum foil, before being thinly dusted with powdered sugar. The coating of butter and sugar will keep the Stollen fresh and moist.

Yule Log

The French Christmas cake called *bûche de Noël* in France is always made from a light sponge sheet filled with a chocolate-, coffee-, or nut-flavored buttercream. The log is garnished with the widest variety of decorations: sometimes chocolate leaves, sometimes green holly leaves, or—as shown in the photograph—meringue mushrooms.

For the sponge layer
8 egg yolks
½ cup (100 g) sugar
1 large pinch of salt
Grated rind of 1 lemon
5 egg whites
¾ cup, roughly (100 g), flour
3 tablespoons (20 g) cornstarch

For the buttercream
1½ cups (300 g) sugar
½ cup (⅛ L) water
7 egg yolks
3 ounces (70 g) good-quality semisweet chocolate
1¾ cups (400 g) butter
½ cup, generous (50 g), cocoa

For the garnish
Marzipan leaves
Meringue mushrooms

Stir together the egg yolks with 1 tablespoon sugar, the salt, and the lemon rind; the mixture should be smooth but not frothy or over-aerated.

Beat the egg whites with the remaining sugar. Fold the egg yolk mixture into the stiffly beaten whites.

Combine the flour and cornstarch, sift, and carefully stir into the mixture.

Preheat the oven to 425°F. (240°C).

Line a baking sheet with parchment paper or silicone paper and spread the batter evenly over it, preferably with an offset-blade spatula or a cake cutter. Bake on the center shelf of the oven for about 8-10 minutes, but check after 6 minutes to be sure the sponge layer is not becoming too dark. When the sponge layer is done, turn it out onto a damp cloth and allow to cool, covered with another cloth.

Boil the sugar and water to the soft-ball stage (240°F./116°C; see page 7). Beat the egg yolks until very light and foamy, then trickle the sugar syrup down the side of the bowl in a very thin stream, continuing to beat vigorously as you do so.

Melt the chocolate over hot water in a double boiler or bain-marie arrangement.

Cream the butter with the cocoa and chocolate until very light and combine with the egg yolk mixture. Spread the sponge sheet evenly with half the buttercream, roll up, and very thinly spread the outside with the buttercream.

Spoon the remaining buttercream into a pastry bag fitted with a small star tip and decorate the cake with piped strips of the mixture. The remaining garnish is up to individual fancy.

The log will yield 16-18 individual slices.

Fruit Bread

This is widespread all through what were once the lands of the Suebi and Alemanni (southwestern Germany, Switzerland, and Alsace-Lorraine). Dried pears are commonly available in natural foods stores; they are the fundamental ingredient of this fruit-rich bread, eaten during the Advent and Christmas season. The simplest versions, those made only from pears and a dark bread dough, are eaten spread with butter—unnecessary with the following recipe, which is enriched with various kinds of dried fruit.

For 3-4 loaves
2¾ cups (500 g) dried pears
1 cup, scant (200 g), dried figs
2 cups (300 g) prunes, pitted
2 quarts (2 L) water
1¼ cups (150 g) shelled walnuts
½ cup, heaping (80 g), almonds
¾ cup (150 g) diced candied orange peel
½ cup (100 g) diced candied lemon peel
2 cups (300 g) raisins
1⅓ cups (200 g) currants
1 large pinch each of ground cloves and anise
¼ teaspoon each ground cinnamon, ginger, and salt
6 jiggers (12 cL) Kirschwasser

For the dough
3¼ cups (450 g) flour
1 package active dry yeast
1 cup, scant (¼ L), milk
2 heaping tablespoons (30 g) sugar
½ teaspoon salt

Remove the stems from the pears and figs; place in a bowl with the prunes. Pour the water over the fruit and allow to soften overnight.

Next day, pour off the water; cut the fruit into small dice, and return to the bowl.

Coarsely chop the walnuts and almonds. Add to the diced dried fruit, along with the raisins and currants. Toss together with the seasonings and pour the Kirschwasser over the mixture. Let steep overnight, covered.

Sift the flour into a bowl, make a depression in the center, and sprinkle in the yeast. Dissolve the yeast in the lukewarm milk and sprinkle the surface with flour. Let stand, covered, in a warm place about 15-20 minutes, until small fissures are visible on the surface of the yeast-milk solution.

Add the sugar and salt to the yeast-milk solution and knead to a very firm dough. Let rise for 20-30 minutes, then knead together with the fruit until all ingredients are thoroughly combined. Shape the dough into 3-4 equal-sized loaves.

Line a baking sheet with silicone paper. Place the loaves on it and let rise in a warm place about 2 hours, covered.

Preheat the oven to 425°F. (220°C).

Bake the loaves on the bottom shelf of the preheated oven 10 minutes, then reduce the heat to 350°F. (180°C) and bake until done, another 60 minutes.

Remove from the oven and let cool, either uncovered or covered with parchment paper. Wrap in aluminum foil after not less than 2 days. The loaves will stay fresh, wrapped and stored in a cool place, for 3-4 weeks.

St. Nicholas Breads

These are baked dough figures known in many regions and made for the feast of St. Nicholas. Starting with a ball of dough, first the body is rolled out in a somewhat elongated shape and cut halfway up one side. Make the legs out of this divided part; score marks on the sides for the arms.

The St. Nicholas figures from the Rhineland are somewhat more complicated; often the St. Nicholas is riding on a horse, and the small clay pipes are mandatory.

For 2-4 figures
7-8 cups (1 kg) flour
1 package active dry yeast
2 cups (½ L) milk
½ cup plus 3 tablespoons (150 g) butter
⅔ cup, scant (120 g), sugar
1 teaspoon salt
Grated rind of 1 lemon
2 eggs
2 egg yolks

Sift the flour into a bowl. Make a depression in the center and sprinkle in the yeast. Warm the milk, pour it in, and dissolve the yeast. Sprinkle a little flour over the yeast-milk mixture and let stand, covered, until small fissures are clearly visible on the surface.

Meanwhile, melt the butter, add the sugar, salt, lemon rind, and whole eggs, and stir to combine.

Add this mixture to the yeast-milk solution and beat to form a light, smooth dough. It must be neither too soft nor too firm and must be easy to shape. Let rise for 15-20 minutes.

The figures are each shaped from a smoothly rounded ball of dough which is first rolled out into a slightly elongated shape. Next the head is shaped. The arms, legs, and hat are attached with egg yolk beaten with a little water. The remaining decorations, such as the beard, nose, eyes, and so forth are shaped or cut out separately and likewise attached with egg yolk.

Preheat the oven to 375°F. (190°C).

Lay the figures on a baking sheet lined with silicone paper and let rise completely (at least 20-25 minutes). Bake on the center shelf of the preheated oven for 20-35 minutes, depending on size.

Panettone

A tale like something from Grimm is told concerning the origin of this Italian Christmas bread: In Milan there once lived a poor pastry-cook with a fabulously beautiful daughter whom he watched over like the apple of his eye. A noble youth by the name of Ughetto della Tella also found the fair Adalgisa toothsome. To win her, he entered into her father's service and became a confectioner in his shop. He won the old man's good graces when he invented a Christmas cake that made the trio rich (and forever famous) overnight: the world-renowned panettone.

The characteristic shape of the cake often presents difficulties—at least outside of Italy, since the correct baking mold is not available. But it can be baked in a ring-shaped or springform pan with no loss of quality or flavor; or use a saucepan of the right size.

For 1 loaf
5 cups (650 g) flour
1 package active dry yeast
1 cup (¼ L) milk
¾ cup plus 2 tablespoons (200 g) butter
¾ cup (150 g) sugar
1 level teaspoon salt
Grated rind of 1 lemon
1 large pinch of nutmeg
6 egg yolks
⅓ cup, generous (80 g), diced candied orange peel
½ cup (100 g) diced candied lemon peel
1 cup (150 g) raisins
⅔ cup (80 g) chopped blanched almonds

Sift the flour into a bowl. Make a depression in the center, sprinkle in the yeast, and dissolve it in the lukewarm milk. Sprinkle a little flour over the yeast-milk mixture and let stand 15-20 minutes, until small fissures are clearly visible on the surface.

Melt the butter and add the sugar, flavorings, and egg yolks. Beat this mixture until somewhat light and frothy, add to the yeast-milk solution, and stir to form a smooth, light dough until blisters form. Let rise 20 minutes, covered.

Combine the candied orange and lemon peel with the raisins and almonds and knead into the dough. Let rise once more in a warm place for 15-20 minutes, covered with a cloth.

Line a baking sheet with silicone paper and place a baking ring on it. Line the edges of the ring with lightly buttered parchment paper and turn out the dough into it. Let rise again 20-25 minutes.

Preheat the oven to 375°F. (190°C).

Bake the cake on the bottom shelf of the oven for 80-90 minutes. Check with a wooden pick to see whether the cake is baked all the way through; no dough should cling to the surface.

Tip: Panettone is not a durable bread meant for extended storage, but a breakfast loaf for feast days. However, an unsliced loaf can be kept for a fairly long while if wrapped in foil, or brushed with an apricot glaze and iced with fondant.

For the latter process, ¼ cup (50 g) of sugar is boiled with 2 jiggers (4 cL) water and 1 teaspoon lemon juice until the sugar is completely dissolved and the mixture is clear. Add a scant ⅓ cup (100 g) apricot preserves and cook about 4-5 minutes, stirring. Brush the panettone with this hot apricot glaze and allow to dry for 10 minutes. Meanwhile, melt the fondant, thin if necessary with egg white or lemon juice, and thinly spread the cake with it.

Gingerbread House

For one house
3 cups, generous (1 kg), honey
1 cup (¼ L) water
½ cup (125g) butter
6 cups (650 g) light rye flour
4 cups (600 g) white flour
½ cup (100 g) finely diced candied lemon peel
½ cup (100 g) finely diced candied orange peel
6 teaspoons ground cinnamon
1¾ teaspoons ground cardamom
1 teaspoon ground cloves
1¼ teaspoons ground ginger
2 tablespoons plus 1 teaspoon (30 g) baking soda
2 egg whites
3½ cups (300 g) powdered sugar
2 tablespoons lemon juice
Colored sugar sprinkles or nonpareils
Almonds and candied cherries

Bring the honey, water, and butter to the boil, stirring; let cool.

Sift the flour onto a pastry board and scatter the candied lemon and orange peel and spices over it. Make a depression in the center and pour in the almost completely cooled honey. Knead these ingredients to a smoothly elastic dough, then thoroughly work the soda into the dough. Let the dough rest overnight, covered, in refrigerator.

It is best to cut out cardboard patterns for the gingerbread house. With these, you can put together a test house that can be altered if you don't like it. See diagram for dimensions.

Preheat the oven to 400°F. (200°C).

For the front of the house roll out 25 ropes ⅜ inch (1 cm) thick and 11 inches (27 cm) long. Lay them next to each other leaving a little room in between each (they will bake together creating a log cabin effect) on a butter baking sheet. Lay the cardboard pattern over the "logs" and pre-cut the front (do not cut out the door and window at this time). Repeat the same procedure for the back of the house and the sides. For the sides, roll out 6 ropes ⅜ inch (1 cm) thick and 8 inches (20 cm) long. You may have to use several baking sheets, or if you only have one, bake as many parts of the house at one time as you can. Bake on center shelf until nicely browned, 15 to 20 minutes. Loosen dough from baking sheet. For front of the house cut out the window and door while still warm (the doors will be set in place and reattached later). Let all pieces cool thoroughly before assembly.

For the roof and the base, roll out the dough no more than ³⁄₁₆ inch (½ cm) to the approximate size of each. Pre-cut the dough using pattern and transfer to buttered baking sheet. Pierce at 1-inch (2½-cm) intervals with a fork, and bake about 12 to 15 minutes on the center shelf until brown.

The picket fence and the rectangular roof decorations (see photo) can be rolled out somewhat thinner, pre-cut and baked in the same fashion as the roof and base. (Use your imagination and create your own designs for the remaining dough.)

Mix the egg whites and powdered sugar to form a thick icing; thin with a little lemon juice if necessary. Use icing to "glue" the house together. The roof should be attached with a few toothpicks. Put remaining icing in a pastry bag fitted with a fine tip, and decorate the house with this and with colored sugar sprinkles, almonds, candied cherries.

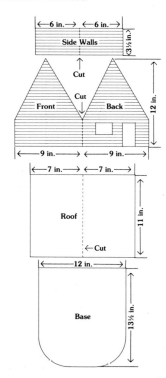

CONVERSION TABLES

Recipes in this book feature customary U.S. measurements. Cooks in other English-speaking countries should follow the metric measurements instead. Do not mix metric measures with U.S. customary measures, since they are not interchangeable. The following measurements may be of additional help:

1 U.S. cup = 8 fluid ounces or 236 mL
1 Imperial pint = 2½ U.S. cups

4 U.S. tablespoons = 3½ Imperial tablespoons
  3 Australian tablespoons
1 jigger = 1½ fluid ounces or 2 U.S. tablespoons

Oven Temperatures

Gas Mark	¼	2	4	6	8
Fahrenheit	225	300	350	400	450
Celsius	110	150	180	200	230

SOURCE LIST

Some of these recipes use ingredients that may not be readily available. They are all available through mail order, however, so we provide a brief list of sources. Items such as *oblaten* (German baking wafers), nougat spread, vanilla sugar, and potassium carbonate are often found in specialty food stores and gourmet shops, particularly ones dealing with German products.

For ingredients
Bremen House, 218 East 86 Street, New York, New York 10028

Karl Ehmer Quality Meats, 63–35 Fresh Pond Road, Ridgewood, New York 11385
Paprikas Weiss, 1546 Second Avenue, New York, New York 10028

For utensils and baking equipment
Bridge Kitchenware Corp., 214 East 52 Street, New York, New York 10022
Maid of Scandinavia, 3244 Raleigh Avenue, Minneapolis, Minnesota 55416

INDEX

Christian Teubner has been for many years a highly sought-after photographer specializing in gastronomy. In his studio for food photography originate masterworks in the shape of culinary photographs, and from his test kitchens come tempting creations in the shape of new recipes. Christian Teubner's work conveys something special wherever food and drink are the subject at hand. In this book, he brings together the tastes and times of an Old World Christmas. For many readers, these recipes will bring to mind the holiday celebrations of an earlier time; for others, they will be exciting new treats for a contemporary celebration.